The Original
I CHING

T0357337

MARGARET J. PEARSON, PH.D.

Foreword by John S. Major, translator of the *Huainanzi*

The Original
I CHING

A LANDMARK TRANSLATION OF
THE BOOK OF CHANGES
BASED ON RECENT DISCOVERIES

TUTTLE Publishing

Tokyo | Rutland, Vermont | Singapore

Published by Tuttle Publishing, an imprint of Periplus Editions (HK) Ltd.

www.tuttlepublishing.com

Copyright © 2025 Margaret J. Pearson

Library of Congress Cataloging-in-Publication Data

Yi jing. English
The original I ching : an authentic translation of The book of changes / by Margaret J. Pearson Ph.D. -- 1st ed.
    256 p. ; 21 cm.
Includes bibliographical references.
ISBN 978-0-8048-4181-8 (hardcover)
I. Pearson, Margaret. II. Title.
PL2478.D58 2011
299'.51282--dc22

                                    2011010712

ISBN 978-0-8048-5738-3
(Previously 978-0-8048-4181-8)

Distributed by

North America, Latin America & Europe
Tuttle Publishing
364 Innovation Drive
North Clarendon, VT 05759-9436 U.S.A.
Tel: (802) 773-8930
Fax: (802) 773-6993
info@tuttlepublishing.com
www.tuttlepublishing.com

Asia Pacific
Berkeley Books Pte. Ltd.
3 Kallang Sector
#04-01, Singapore 349278
Tel: (65) 6741-2178
Fax: (65) 6741-2179
inquiries@periplus.com.sg
www.tuttlepublishing.com

First edition
29 28 27 26 25   5 4 3 2 1

Printed in Singapore   2410TP

Frontispiece: The history official Ban Zhao (d. 116) lecturing to her students. A great scholar, she worked in the imperial history bureau and taught palace ladies and the scholar Ma Jung (d. 166). Ma and his student Zheng Xuan (d. 200) were among China's greatest exegetes. Some of his footnotes have been used in preparing this translation.

This is one of the few extant pictures of a woman scholar in early China. The painting is an early copy of an original attributed to Gu Kaizhi (d. 406). This image is from a photograph of the entire scroll by Benrido, Japan in 1965, and published in 1966 by the Trustees of the British Museum.

To Phyllis Pearson, my mother and first teacher

and to Jean Musser, who introduced me to Chinese literature,
and Professor Carol Thomas, who has advised me
since I began my doctoral studies

Contents

Foreword

Of the vast library of classical Chinese texts, most Westerners recognize only three: Sunzi's *Art of War*, Laozi's *Tao Te Ching* (*Daodejing*), and *The Book of Changes* (*I Ching* or *Yijing*). (Confucius is widely recognized by name, but few non-specialists are familiar with the Analects, the compendium of his teachings.) The I Ching, like the *Art of War* and the *Tao Te Ching*, has been translated dozens of times in many different languages. So it is reasonable to ask: Does the world need another translation of the *Book of Changes*? The answer is yes, if it adds to our understanding of this much-studied text. Margaret Pearson's translation does just that.

This is a very unusual book. Most translations of the *I Ching* are either scholarly works for an academic audience or popular versions that take the text as a kind of fortune-telling manual. The academic translations tend to treat the *I Ching* as a cultural-historical phenomenon, paying little attention to how a reader might actually consult the text. The popular translations too often are pastiches by writers whose grasp of Classical Chinese is shaky or non-existent, producing versions that are not well grounded in early Chinese cultural history. And almost all translations of the *I Ching* have been done by men whose approach to the text often is influenced by subtle, or sometimes not-so-subtle, masculine bias. Margaret Pearson's work breaks the mold. A distinguished professor emerita of East Asian history at Skidmore College, she combines a rigorous reading of the oldest layer of the *I Ching*'s text with a modern gender-neutral perspective. The result is an accurate and reliable translation that is focused on how to use The Book of Changes as a guide to thinking through the questions that inevitably arise in the course if our lives.

In digging down to the mother lode of ancient text, Pearson removes the overburden of commentary that is found in all standard editions of the *I Ching*. The original text that accompanied the sixty-four hexagrams is known as the *Chou i* (*Zhouyi*), ("The Zhou [dynasty] Book of Changes"). Often abstruse or enigmatic, it early on attracted the attention of scholars who wrote commentaries to explain the meaning (as they perceived it) of the hexagrams, or of the individual lines that comprise them. That was mostly a good thing—the ancient line and hexagram texts certainly require explanation. But as a certain set of commentaries, known as the "Ten Wings," was favored by the thinkers of the Song dynasty (10th-13th centuries CE) as being compatible with the prevailing current of Neo-Confucian philosophy, explanation hardened into orthodoxy, narrowing the range of possible interpretations of the text.

In China in former times (like all known ancient civilizations, and to a surprising degree still today) patriarchy was woven into the fabric of everyday life. Yet in very ancient times there was some scope for female agency, and early historical accounts portray some elite women as taking charge of their own lives. The words *yin* and *yang*, which later became cosmological paradigms of gender difference, signified "the shady side of a hill or riverbank) (*yin*) or "the sunny side..." (*yang*), reflecting the fact that the hexagrams of the *Zhouyi*, like the oracle-bone texts of the preceding Shang dynasty, were deeply concerned with weather, climate, agriculture, and related subjects.

The scope of agency available to women began to narrow in the late Warring States and early Han periods (3rd – 1st centuries BCE), as both new cosmological theories and formulations of social philosophy had the effect of bolstering gender (and other) hierarchies. But society still offered some scope for elite women. Intellectuals of that era may have preferred *yang* (now endowed with qualities like male, bright, hot, dry, etc.) over yin (female, dark, cool, moist, etc.), but most schools of thought acknowledged that both were inseparable and essential. A book from the 1st century BCE called the *Lieh nü chuan* (*Lie nu zhuan*, "Accounts of Exemplary Women") held up as role models women who were famous for their modesty, chastity, and obedience (but one wonders how many young women were secretly inspired by its chapter on bad examples, which profiles women who were far more lively and interesting than their virtuous sisters.)

As late as the Tang dynasty (7th-10th centuries CE), some elite women played polo, wrote poetry, and actively participated in social life. Ladies at court wore the latest fashions, which the men predictably hated (the famous poet Po Chü-I (Bai Juyi) complained, "Our women are dressing like foreigners' wives,") Some women found fulfillment as Buddhist or Daoist nuns; abesses sometimes were part of the power structure at the local level.

With the rise of Neo-Confucianism in the 10th century, that changed. The feminine *yin* was demonized; men cultivated their yang masculinity. The dualistic perspective of *yin* and *yang* that they represent was baked into the commentarial tradition that grew up around the *Book of Changes*. Elite women were increasingly confined to the "women's quarters" in the inner courtyards of their homes. It is no accident that the practice of footbinding originated at that time. And the masculine bias of the *I Ching* commentaries fit the mold; androcentrism curdled into misogyny.

Liberated from the orthodoxy of the commentaries, the original *Zhouyi* text opens to admit other interpretations. Although the actors portrayed in the text have traditionally been assumed to be male, the brief, cryptic image texts and line texts are often not explicitly gendered, giving a translator leeway to employ gender-neutral language in her translation. You do not need to identify as female to use this translation as the basis for consulting the *I Ching*; you only need an open mind.)

A s the traditional commentaries can be peeled off the original ancient text, advances in archaeology have given us new information about that ur-text, and new ways of reading it. Beginning in the final third of the twentieth century, and continuing to the present day, China has experienced a golden age of archaeology that has had a transformative effect on the study of early Chinese history. In addition to treasures of bronze and jade, and terra-cotta warriors, hundreds of manuscripts written on pieces of silk cloth or on long strips of bamboo have emerged from tombs dating from several centuries BCE. Many of these are works previously unknown, or known only by title, the content having long since been lost. Others are early versions of texts that were handed down through the ages, but with passages that are sometimes quite different from the versions of the received tradition. Among the latter are two versions of the *I Ching* dating from the 2nd century BCE. The Shanghai Museum bamboo-strip text and the Mawangdui silk text both have passages that are significantly different from the familiar received text. This doesn't mean that the received text is always "wrong"; rather it shows that the text had not yet become stabilized, and variant hand-written versions of the text (this was long before the invention of printing) were in circulation at the time. But in some cases the received text had characters that did not make much sense, even by the enigmatic standards of the *I Ching*, and the newly discovered texts have a character in the same place that fits much better. So the puzzling character turns out to be a scribal error that can be corrected by comparison with the bamboo and silk versions. In what from an academic point of view is the most radical aspect of Pearson's translation, she uses the archaeologically-discovered Mawangdui silk text to propose corrected readings for some puzzling characters. This openness to the fruits of up-to-date scholarship makes her translation all the more valuable.

So this book is based on some heavyweight academic work, but the book itself is not heavy; on the contrary, one of the best things about it is that it is very reader-friendly. This is a version of the *I Ching* that is intended to be used. In a clear but meticulously detailed chapter, "How to Use the Book of Changes," she explains how to consult the *I Ching* in a way that provides insight into decisions you have to make, or problems that are troubling you.

The first step is to ask the right kind of question. The *I Ching* is not designed to answer questions with a simple "yes" or "no." The question should allow for ambiguity, plusses and minuses, advantages and disadvantages, and reasonably admit more than one possible answer. Then, to get started, you need to generate a hexagram, and Pearson explains exactly how to do that, tossing three coins simultaneously six times to build a stack of solid or broken lines. (In a further step, which does not always occur, "weak" lines in the original hexagram are changed to "strong" lines, yielding a new, second hexagram. (This procedure is probably the reason why this text is called *The Book of Changes*). Then the work begins. Pearson lays out a procedure rather reminiscent of journal-keeping, which encourages you to record in writing your immediate, instinctive response to your hexagram, and then write down your orderly, considered response to the six individual lines. The process continues through several iterations, in the course of which you challenge your earlier impressions and assumptions. You will also want to read and reflect on Pearson's own deeply perceptive and personal comments on the hexagrams. As you work through the process, an answer to your question will emerge—not "yes" or "no," but a nuanced piece of advice. Then you make your decision, which might even be to ignore the oracle's message. But you will have confidence that at least you have delved deeply into the implications of your question.

As you become accustomed to using the *I Ching* in this way, you will find that it is a helpful and reliable companion on your journey through life. Margaret Pearson's insightful and reliable translation of the ancient text is a good place to start.

—John S. Major

Acknowledgments

"If you want to see far, it is better to climb a hill than to stand on your toes." Xunzi wrote this, probably not long before China was first unified in 221 BCE, and it remains true today. I could never have attempted this translation without the resources and insights provided by other scholars, most notably Lou Yulie, K.C. Chang, Richard John Lynn, Edward Shaughnessy, and David Keightley.

Several scholarly communities supported this endeavor. Clare Hall, Cambridge University, welcomed me as a Visiting Fellow in 1997, thanks to the sponsorship of Michael Loewe and the support of David Knechtges. Many sections of this work were first presented to the Clare Hall Women's Group, where I received warm support, especially from Asian women scholars. Professor Xinzhong Yao was one of the first to recognize the importance of this difficult task.

My first effort, to translate hexagram 44, was presented at one of the text reading seminars of the Needham Research Institute. I am grateful for the comments I received there, especially from Professors Michael Nylan and Michael Loewe. Mark Lewis, then at Cambridge University, validated my first tentative reinterpretations of key passages. Professor Lynn gave me helpful and encouraging comments on my analysis of hexagram 44, first published in *Oracle: the Journal of Yijing Studies* (London, 2000). The Needham Research Institute provided office space and intellectual community over several years, while I worked on the life of the great Chinese scientist Zhang Heng. In 2005, I led a discussion of his use of the *Changes* at another text reading there. In the past few years, membership in the Early China Seminar at Columbia University, capably led by Li Feng and David Branner, enabled me to continue to learn more about the best recent scholarship on early China and its texts.

In preparing the translations, I have relied on the work of many other scholars. My primary Chinese sources include Lou Yulieh's *Critical edition of the Works of Wang Bi with explanatory notes* (*Wang Bi ji jiaoshi,* Beijing, 1980), an inspiring breakthrough in *Yijing* studies, for he pruned away many commentaries and focused attention on the oldest portions of the text, usually referred to as the Zhou *Changes* (or *Zhouyi*). This edition also helped distinguish between *Zhouyi* and later versions, and separated Wang Bi's contributions from others'. I also used Guo Linzong's *Paihua Yijing* (Taipei, 1999). which was also based on this text. Two Chinese-Chinese dictionaries published in the 1990s were particularly helpful: the *Zhouyi Dacidian* (Canton, 1993) and Liu Xinlong's *Xin pien jiaguwen zidian* (Beijing, 1993). The first provided meanings only from *Yijing, Shijing, Zuozhuan,* and other early works, a very welcome tool for etymological focus. The second provided beautiful images and interpretations of the earliest forms of crucial characters. While some of Liu's conclusions may be controversial, given the fragmentary nature of the evidence he used, I consider most of them valid alternatives, and have used them here.

For an understanding of the changing nature of *yin,* I am particularly grateful for the pioneering work of Vitaly A. Rubin (1982), Alison Black (1989), and Lisa Raphals (1998). Conversations with Professor Nylan at Clare Hall in 2005 encouraged this revisionist approach. I believe that her chapter on *yin/yang* thought in the revised *Cambridge History of China* for the Qin and Han eras supports the general direction described by Raphals, Black, and Rubin which I have used as the rationale for this translation. This does not mean, however, that these scholars have reviewed this translation or would agree with every word of it. At the annual meeting of the American Oriental Society in 2010, I presented my arguments on the positive and ungendered meaning of *yin*. I am grateful for the comments from my listeners there.

Early stages of this twelve-year project received financial support from Skidmore College and the Mellon Foundation. Fongyee Walker provided useful information on terms and images common to both *Yijing* and *Shijing*, the subject of her research at Cambridge University. John Moffett generously shared his knowledge of the *Zuozhuan* and of the many women involved in divination depicted in this late Zhou text. Sally Church helped in many ways, particularly with early drafts on *yin*. Elizabeth Childs-Johnson, Constance Cook, and Anne Kinney reviewed drafts of the introduction. Jeff Howard reviewed the entire manuscript and helped in many ways, as he did with my dissertation. These scholars have helped me identify mistakes and infelicities. Those that remain are mine alone.

Helmut Wilhelm, Jack Dull, and Hok-lam Chan guided my first steps into sinology as a graduate student at the University of Washington. Carol Thomas led me towards valid cross-cultural comparisons with early Greek history. Her tact and scholarly expertise also enabled me to complete my doctoral dissertation that included the first translation of another early Chinese text into any language. Most recently, the skillful editing of Michael Ochs and the support of my scholarly friend Carol Ochs have been crucial in bringing this task to completion.

I am indebted to the thousands of students I have taught over the last thirty years, and particularly to the hundreds introduced to the *Changes* in a course I taught every year. The papers they wrote relating what they learned from the *Changes* to their own lives and dilemmas have taught me much. Particular thanks go to the students who helped me revise the instructions for consulting the book.

I have been fortunate to learn much from many, but I am also quite aware that I have probably made errors, an inescapable reality in the difficult task of reinterpreting a text nearly three thousand years after its creation. While I have tried to emulate the work of my former teacher Burton Watson and of D. C. Lau, their scholarship is greater than mine, as is their command of English precisely suited to accurately conveying Chinese thought. I have dared to undertake this task in large part because I believe that all women who read the *Changes* deserve at least one translation by a woman scholar with knowledge of Chinese language and history. And, of course, I welcome suggestions for improving the text. As Confucius said, when I am in a group of three, I always have two teachers.

Introduction

The *Book of Changes (I Ching* or *Yijing)* is unlike any other book in its structure and its origins, yet its purpose is universal: to provide good counsel to its users in making the decisions that respond to and create change. As such, it has become a compendium of wisdom used by people of many cultures and eras.

The text is very old, and it is closely associated with the Zhou dynasty, founded around 1050 BCE. The earliest core text, translated here, is, therefore, usually referred to as the Zhou *Changes (Zhouyi)*, to differentiate it from the later, longer work, elaborated and developed with multiple commentaries and addenda, representing centuries of efforts to fully comprehend the meaning of the core text. However, the text also includes phrases used in earlier divinations by the preceding Shang dynasty (circa 1600–1050? BCE). More on this history below.

In structure, the book has sixty-four sections, each associated with a six-line figure (hexagram) of solid and broken lines. This figure is named, and represents both a human situation and an object. The reader is encouraged to see similarities between the two, a type of reasoning which is discussed below.

Each hexagram is composed of two three-line figures (trigrams), which represent natural objects: sky, earth, wind, mountain, water, thunder, fire, and lake. Immediately following the name are one or more brief statements that are generally referred to as "judgments"; these are followed by brief statements associated with changing lines. Most statements have words of advice appended, such as "misfortune," "good fortune," "this is effective," or "this is not effective." Finally, there is a brief "image" (*xiang*).

The book has been used for millennia for both decision-making and as a basis for philosophical speculation. Its concepts undergird most of East Asian thought and had a profound influence on the theories of Carl Jung and his followers. In various forms, it is consulted by Asians and westerners, in temples, homes, and therapists' offices. Its study remains a mainstay of attempts to understand Chinese culture.

Thus this book is neither purely prophetic nor purely philosophical. While its appropriate use has been controversial for centuries, common sense suggests that no major decision should be made on the basis of the advice of any one person or book. However, over the centuries, many have found that consulting the *Changes* can encourage thoughtful decision-makers to see aspects of situations to which they had been blind. The natural images in the *Changes*, when considered as analogous to recurring human situations, can provide fruitful images for meditation as people search for ways through—or out of—their specific dilemmas.

So, consulting or meditating on parts of the *Changes* can function as part of the endless quest for knowledge of the self and of others, which, as Confucian philosopher Xunzi declared, is what makes us fully human. It can also provide practical knowledge that leads to action. Well-considered and timely actions are more likely to help work toward a more gracefully ordered set of sociological systems. Therefore, the wisdom of the *Changes*, properly used, can lead us toward a life that is "refined in purpose, pure in virtuous understanding," and that allows us "to live in the present and derive our purposes from [understanding] the past," according to Xunzi.

The *Changes* expresses a belief that different conditions require different responses, and that we are never entirely alone, that is, never free of some social context. Some things are within our power to decide while others are not. It is as though we were each born into a different portion of the river so that history, culture, our time, and our place are blended. We can rarely change the speed or direction of the river of history. Such changes can occur only naturally or with the combined forces of many people. Nevertheless, we must each paddle our own canoe so that through trial and error we learn to adapt to different situations. We learn to be attentive to various factors in various situations, to act, to react, or not to act at all, as appropriate. Paddling through a calm stretch is quite different from paddling through rapids. We learn to listen for the sounds of what lies ahead: to recognize the sound of a waterfall before we have reached it.

The *Changes* was designed to help leaders, and its readers, make more informed decisions. Used appropriately, it can help us see aspects of a situation which we may have ignored. It cannot make our decisions for us any more than any one expert can solve all our problems. But it provides fruitful images for us to ponder at times of stress. In some odd way (Jung called it synchronicity), it may provide insights suitable for the time. It is not necessary to believe in magic or fortune telling to derive benefit from using this book. In fact, it is best used as part of a thoughtful process involving repeated meditation, journaling, and the advice of others. It was not intended to replace moral dicta but to assist those determined to act responsibly. It can prod us toward a deeper, more informed view of the world and our actions within it.

This new version of the text provides a fresh translation that is faithful to the oldest layer of the text but comprehensible to the non-specialist. It aims to be as clear or as vague as the text itself, and to provide just enough background information to help readers make some sense of it. For those who want more information, a list of some good places to begin is provided. You are encouraged to compare this translation with others to help discern the meaning of the original Chinese text behind both versions more clearly. Included also are a number of ways of reading the book that some people have found useful. My hope is that publishing this translation will achieve what the book itself tries to foster: wise choices, consideration of others as well as the whole of oneself, and efforts to encourage both justice and mercy wherever we may be.

History of the Text

The origins of this book are Chinese, a culture where leaders regularly sought insight on policy decisions through divination—the practice of foretelling the future by interpreting signs or omens. This is a sharp contrast with Judeo-Christian culture, which was founded on belief in an omniscient deity which told humans precisely what we should and should not do, in messages like the Ten Commandments. Divination also existed in ancient Greece and Rome, where the entrails of sacrificial animals were analyzed, and oracles were consulted, at Delphi, in Siwah (by Alexander the Great). However, in the post-pagan west, it has been outlawed since Israel was first united, under King Saul. This mistrust of divination and diviners continues: in Canada, New York, and other states, it is a crime to accept money for divination, except as entertainment.

Ancient China had no tradition of a god who spoke clearly, giving words and laws to prophets. Instead, early rulers used other methods to determine what they should do.

During the Shang dynasty (circa 1600–1050? BCE), rulers sought divine counsel by having specialists inscribe questions on turtle shells and ox scapulae, use heat to create cracks, and interpret the cracks as answers.[1] Such answers were unclear, so some

---

1.   For examples of Shang divination, see Keightley (1999).

diviners kept the bones and shells and added notes on what actually happened, as a way of learning to improve the accuracy of their readings. These are our first historical records from China. They also point to another Chinese method of discovering what we should do: studying history to see what happened to people who made different decisions, or the same decisions under different conditions.

When the Zhou (Chou) people overthrew the Shang (1050? BCE), they kept some of the sacrificial religious and political rituals and methods of divination but they added another form of divination, using the tossing of yarrow stalks instead of the burning and cracking of bones and shells. Some of the formulae of Shang divination continued, and the questions continued to be binary in form.[2] Eventually Zhou divinations were collected into a book, the Zhou *Changes* (*Zhouyi*). A text with this name existed and was consulted by Zhou rulers, their advisors, and others in later eras. Women as well as men used it.[3]

---

2. Inscriptions on Shang oracle bones and turtle plastrons usually state the same question twice, once positively and once negatively. For example, in the format: "Will doing the sacrifice to Mother Xi on the third day be auspicious? Will doing the sacrifice to Mother Xi on the third day not be auspicious?" or "Would attacking our threatening neighbor state X next month be a disaster? Would attacking our threatening neighbor state X next month not be a disaster?"

    In addition, some terms used on both oracle bones and in the *Zhouyi* express opposites: good fortune and misfortune; danger, no danger; blame, no blame; persisting is effective or not.

    Leibnitz and others have remarked upon the binary nature of hexagram lines; that is, either broken or unbroken. Because computer instructions are, at base, binary, some find deep significance in this. However, there are actually four possibilities for every line: 6, 7, 8, and 9. Only sixes and nines are discussed in the *Zhouyi*, and both of these are in the process of changing from broken to solid or solid to broken. For more information, see the section "How to Use the *Book of Changes*." One of Wang Bi's revisions was referring to changing lines as types of *yin* or *yang* rather than just the original six or nine. This makes it seem as though these concepts pervade the text, although the character for *yin* actually appears only once in the core *Zhouyi*.

3. For samples of Zhou divination, see *Tso chuan*. For a list of these examples, see Moffett.

The *Changes* became one of the five classics,[4] literally the warp of Chinese culture from the era of Confucius until the elimination of the imperial civil service examinations in 1905. Thus the book is also a window into the most basic and pervasive attitudes within east Asian cultures. It is, however, also hard to understand. It is both laconic and so ancient that we cannot be sure that we know what the words meant when it was created long ago. By 150 CE educated Chinese scholars had begun to use their first etymological dictionary to help them make sense of it and other early works.

Many commentaries have been written on the *Yijing*, and the text we know today consists of many layers of these commentaries and images. These commentaries were written and later printed on the same page as the text itself, though usually in smaller characters. Some of these notes clarified basic meanings, while others provided complex theoretical theories. The two types of comments were not differentiated or printed as separate books. Most readers relied on the work of earlier scholars to make any sense of the basic text at all. Thus the meaning of various passages evolved over time, though such an evolution was rarely acknowledged. Scholars and readers tended to use the whole corpus to understand the original text, not realizing than an evolution in meaning had occurred.

Many early commentaries have been lost, and only fragments remain, embodied in later comments. For example, we know little

---

4.   Originally there were six classics: the Book of History (*Shujing*), Book of Poetry (*Shijing*), Book of Music (*Yuejing*), Spring and Autumn Annals (*Qunqiu*), Book of Rites (*LiJi*), and the Book of Changes (*Yijing*). The Book of Music was lost at an early stage. Later, the Analects (*Lunyu*) of Confucius and the Mencius (by Mencius) were added to this list. There are varying definitions of the numbers and names of the Chinese classics over the centuries, but these five have been included in virtually every list. They functioned as the warp of the culture, holding its values. Much philosophical discourse was expressed in commentaries on the classics. For more information, see Michael Nylan, *The Five "Confucian" Classics* (listed in Further Reading).

of the once important school of Jing Fang except that he empha-
sized the images (*xiang*), as this version does, and that his interpretations were popular among great skeptical scholars like Zhang
Heng in the second century CE.

The oldest complete extant commentary on the *Changes* is by
Wang Bi (d. 249 CE). However, Wang Bi lived about a thousand
years after the *Changes* was created, in a world that was pro-
foundly different. We now know much more about early China
than he or Confucius did, thanks to the work of archaeologists
and scholars, especially in the last few decades. Unlike them, we
can read translations of Shang oracle bones instead of relying
only on traditions and texts distorted by copying and recopying.
And we know far more about early China.

This translation is based on this new knowledge, which includes a new awareness of the powers held by some elite women
in early China. In the section "Understanding the Context of the
Book of Changes" we will consider some of these new understand-
ings within the historical context of the Zhou period.

Why This Translation? Yin/Yang and Gender

Wang Bi wrote his commentary based on the assumption that the
paired concepts of *yin* and *yang* were gendered and existed at the
time the *Book of Changes* was created, and that these concepts are
expressed throughout the book, so that every solid line in the hexagrams represented *yang* and every broken line *yin*. He assumed that
yang represented strength, goodness, and masculinity, and that *yin*
was associated with physical and moral weakness and with women.
Later scholars followed his reasoning. Thus the great Sui-Tang
scholar Kong Yingda (d. 648) believed that a word which means
great elsewhere in the *Changes* means *lascivious* when it applied
to a woman. Although these interpretations have held over the
centuries, and the binary way of viewing the world was eventually embodied in the familiar black and white disk, some scholars

now acknowledge that this approach is anachronistic. The Zhou *Changes*, the oldest layers of the text, are concrete, not abstract.

Furthermore, within the oldest layers of the *Changes* itself, the character *yang* does not appear at all, and the character *yin* appears only once: "Cranes sing out from yin ... their young respond" (hexagram 61). Here, *yin* is apparently the place where the nest is located. (More on this below.) We cannot even conclude that *yin* is gendered by association with the parent, since both crane parents care for their young, and the text does not indicate either gender or whether the words are singular or plural. *Yin* and *yang* do appear as abstractions in the *Great Treatise (Dazhuan)*, but even in this important commentary on the *Changes* from the third-century BCE, a relatively late date, they are not gendered. The gendered *yin/yang* interpretation by Wang Bi in the third century CE is an anachronistic addition to the text, even though it is the earliest extant complete commentary. However, most translators seem to be unaware of this. Richard Lynn has done a great service to the field by translating the whole of Wang Bi's commentary, and by carefully distinguishing between the Zhou *Changes*, Wang Bi's, and other commentaries. He has also selected some of the most helpful of many later commentaries. For this reason, I have included references to his work below mine.

The character *yin* has the radical (or categorical symbol) for a hill, not the radical used for women. *Yin*'s earliest forms show a bird and a hill: 𨸏 The hill is still the radical for this character, indicating its original meaning was topographic, not gendered. Other meanings for *yin* given in the *Book of Songs (Shijing)* and *Book of History (Shujing)* include icehouses and the huts in which new kings mourned their fathers. All imply refuge or shelter from the implacable sun of the north China plain, or, by analogy, from pressure to make decisions.

While Wang Bi referred to changing lines as *yin* and *yang*, the original Zhou *Changes* do not. Instead, they are referred to as sixes or nines, that is, lines in transition from strength (solidity) to weakness (broken) or from extreme weakness to strength. Thus the original text recognized the fluid nature of change, the subject of the book as a whole.

Most current translations render *hou* as "prince, he," just as they translate every gender-neutral word as masculine. To a certain extent this is reasonable, since most who used this book were elite men. But we now know that Shang royal women took part in divinations, and that a number of women consulted or interpreted divinations during the Zhou dynasty. And at least one great lady of the Han Dynasty (206 BCE–220 CE) cared enough about the text that it was interred in her tomb, at Mawangdui. Thanks to the research of Sinologist Lisa Raphals, we also know that women's virtues in early China were as widely construed as those of men, including sagacity as well as the modesty and self-restraint valued for all the fully educated at that time.

Thus the rigidly dichotomous and gendered *yin/yang* analysis of the *Changes* is anachronistic to the era of its creation and earliest use. This is a major justification for seeking a meaning closer to the original, as recent scholars like Shaughnessy have tried to do. I believe we can also benefit from an analytic method that gives increased emphasis to the images, an approach used in the Han dynasty. These sections of the text do not invoke abstract notions of *yin* and *yang*, though parts of the *Ta Chuan*, or *Great Commentary*, do. They reason by analogies between human situations and natural phenomena, likening, for example, friendship to linked lakes in hexagram 58.

Anyone who reads the *Changes* with care will find that the meaning of the text can seem to shift from question to question, and from day to day. In a similar way, if we watch a hillside we will see it shift from mottled darkness to brighter colors during the course of a day. Such dramatic surface changes can be distracting. They should, however, remind us to keep our focus on those realities of hillside or situation which remain constant despite the momentary shifts between darkness and light. That observation is based on this author's photographing sides of rivers and hills in an effort to see more clearly what *yin* and *yang* meant before they were abstracted into black and white portions of a circle. Of course, little in nature is entirely black or white, and the boundaries between the sides of a given hill are not clearly demarcated. When we remember that *yin* and *yang* are north and south sides, both of which receive light and shade during the course of the day, that another word refers to the western side of a hill at dawn, and that there is a plethora of terms for types of shade, shadow, and darkness in Chinese, we can see how oversimplified this well-known symbol is.

Freed from anachronistic *yin/yang* thinking with its overly sweeping generalities, we can now attempt a better understanding of the kinds of wisdom that Zhou *Changes* reveals. We see the concerns of the rulers who first used it in divining the timing, methods, and intensity of offensive and defensive warfare. We can also see the rulers' concerns in coping with times of danger, in building and maintaining alliances, and in the relative wisdom of action or delay. While some of the lines and Chinese characters in the book will always remain debatable, some general attitudes recur, among them: persistence is usually but not always effective; going it alone is sometimes necessary but is never a position of strength (see hexagrams 7, 8, 13, 45, and 49 on gathering supporters before acting); apparent weakness may morph into strength (see hexagrams 3 and 41); and apogees do not last (see whexagrams 1, 28, and 55).

Without the excessive bipolarity of gendered *yin/yang* analysis, natural imagery comes through far more strongly, and we are led back into the evocative analogous thinking of the Classic of Poetry or Book of Odes (the *Shijing*) as well as the *Changes*, as in the full passage from hexagram 61 cited earlier:

Cranes sing out from the southern bank of the river. Their young respond.
I have a good wine container. I will share it with you.

This is not the discursive, carefully explained reasoning with which Westerners are comfortable, but rather the allusive world of poetry and of thinkers like Xunzi and Mencius. Trying to derive meanings divorced from traditional commentaries leaves us on shaky ground: we may well misunderstand. But failing to make this attempt is to lose an incredible wealth of meaning, wisdom, and soul-touching beauty.

So here, based on direct interpretation of the original ancient Chinese text, along with background knowledge of the time's Chinese culture, wildlife, and other context, is a possible interpretation:

Since crane chicks develop their legs before their wings, they are vulnerable to predators for a relatively long period. For this reason, their nests are hidden among the reeds on the southern shore of bodies of water, where, in the northern hemisphere, sunlight is less direct. Here eggs and chicks have more shade than they would on the northern (*yang*) shore. The crane parent(s) call out to the fledgling(s), and the young reply, showing that they are still alive and well, and safely within calling distance of the nest. By crying out, the crane parent calls its young to the refuge of the nest, much as a friend reaches out to another by offering to share something else that is comforting, a goblet of wine. The cry and the proffered cup are reminders of a linkage, and a call to gather again.

A person consulting the *Changes* who was considering whether or not to reach out to an alienated friend or family member could be encouraged by these lines to do so, at least to the extent of the courteous sharing of a drink, meal, or refuge.

A New Reading of the Book of Changes

While the unfortunate, dichotomized *yin/yang* definitions now current in both the West and the East may never fade away, the richer natural imagery that has been obscured by them can invigorate our thinking, help us see beyond conventional divisions, and lead us toward a deeper wisdom, a philosophy perhaps more useful in riding the changes in our own lives and times as well as in interpreting the past.

To unlock the wisdom of the *Changes,* we need the fruits of many fields—archaeology, epigraphy, literary analysis, natural history, history, sinology, and on and on. This effort may have as many problems as those faced by a newly sprouted plant. But it also bears as much promise of rich reward as the long-lived mulberry tree, feeder of silkworms, basis of silk production and all that has meant for the economic strength of China and the Chinese. (See hexagrams 3 and 12 for more on these images.)

Analysis of this multifaceted kind alters our reading of the *Changes.* Hexagram 44 offers a striking example of how the entire meaning of a statement in the *Changes* can be transformed.

The *yin/yang* dichotomy we discussed, which pervades the traditional translations of the *Changes,* poses a particular problem for women consulting hexagram 44. Much evidence supports the idea that the situation depicted in this hexagram relates to a bride born into royalty. The character *hou,* which occurs in hexagram 44, is the key here. Most current translations render *hou* as "prince, he," since as we discussed, every gender-neutral word is translated as masculine. But a recent dictionary of oracle bone characters, Liu Xinglong's *Xin pien jiaguwen zidian* (Beijing, 1993), shows that early forms of the character *hou* depict a woman in the process of giving birth; that is, with the *zi* character for "child," head down, coming out of the character for "woman": 㛼

This is fully consistent with the fertility imagery of hexagram 44 and with the importance of a doubly royal heir to improve the probability of peace within the state and with the state to which it has become allied by marriage.

In the most popular translation, by Richard Wilhelm and Cary F. Baynes, we read this summary of traditional commentaries:

> This hexagram indicates a situation in which the principle of darkness ... furtively and unexpectedly obtrudes again from within and below. Of its own accord the female principle comes to meet the male. It is an unfavorable and dangerous situation and we must understand and promptly prevent the possible consequences ... The rise of the inferior element is pictured here in the image of a bold girl who lightly surrenders herself and thus seizes power. This would not be possible if the strong and light-giving element had not in turn come halfway. The inferior things seems so harmless and inviting that a man delights in it; it looks so small and weak that he imagines he may dally with it and come to no harm.
>
> The inferior man rises only because the superior man does not regard him as dangerous and so lends him power. If he were resisted from the first, he could never gain influence.

This admonition seems to enjoin fear and encourage the persecution of the weak. But the fresh translation presented here directs our attention instead to the positive meaning of a time when two states have achieved peace and sealed the alliance with a marriage linking their ruling families. The woman arriving is the royal bride, and she is honored by a welcoming committee of the highest dignitaries which, like the great "King" Wen, has met her on the road long before she has reached her destination. The pregnancy images in the lines refer to the hope of an heir who will embody this alliance, a doubly royal son with such a strong claim to the succession that civil conflict may be averted.

In this book, a new translation of the judgment and image in hexagram 44 replaces this rather destructive dichotomous thinking (italics represent this author's comments):

> **The royal bride:** The woman is great. Do not grab the woman. *A royal bride was met with great ceremony, not taken by force.*

> **The image.** Below the sky, a wind: the image of the royal bride. [*As gentle and persistent as the wind,*] the queen spreads her influence and makes proclamations which reach the four corners of the world.

The kind of power brought by a royal bride is a gentle, long-term influence similar to that of a steady wind. Such gentle power is brought to fruition with the birth and appropriate rearing of an heir truly worthy of the throne. Thus after many years she may be able to foster a deep and enduring transformation of the country, its people, and its relationships with its neighbors.

In our new understanding of the *Changes,* the natural and human images like those above shine, illuminating our thinking in ways similar to those that Gilbert Murray attributed to the Greek gods, "to whom doubtful philosophers can pray, with all a philosopher's due caution, as to so many radiant and heart-searching hypotheses." The *Changes* may not ask us to pray, but its natural and social images challenge us to envision more effective and productive relationships and interactions, ways of coping with the complexities of a complex political world with both idealism and realism. Perhaps this is one step toward true wisdom.

Understanding the Context
of the Book of Changes

The Eternal Concerns of Timing and Timeliness

Timing and sequence matter. If we get the timing wrong, we court disaster. This can be as simple as missing a deadline. An unfiled tax form on April 18 has repercussions that it did not have on April 10. Likewise, sequence has impact; if you are making a peanut butter sandwich, you need to start by laying down a piece of bread before spreading the peanut butter. If you reverse these two steps, you will have a mess, not a sandwich. Our lives are filled with such sequences. Some are obvious, some are not.

In our lives, there are also some aspects we can control and others we cannot. Each of us is born to a set of parents in a place and time we did not choose. We are born into a given moment in the stream of history and culture. If we can see our historical and social contexts more clearly, we may be able to act more effectively.

The Zhou world lacked our peanut butter sandwiches and complex tax returns but of course it had taxes and food preparation steps. We share the same sequence of seasons and the same inability to make precise predictions about tomorrow's weather. But then, as now, leaders needed to know the relative strengths of their states and armies before they began a war. They needed to make sure good dams were built before heavy rain brought floods.

And they needed to recruit farmers to make dams when they were not needed in the fields for sowing and reaping, lest the whole nation starve.

Different times require different actions. Sometimes they require timely inaction; that is, waiting for a more appropriate time. As adults, we learn when to speak and when to keep silent. We learn that some actions need more preparations than others. In some cases, laws enforce certain sequences: we need to prove we can drive and buy insurance before we can take a car on the road legally. In other cases, courtesy provides guidelines. "Please" and "thank you" ease many interactions and make sharing more likely.

In early China, seasonal changes were an abiding concern. The north China plains are often dry, and the need for rain a persistent anxiety.[5] This is reflected in ancient poems[6] and in many passages about thunder and rain in the *Changes*. Invasion by nomadic tribes or neighboring states was another persistent threat. But going to war prematurely was a greater danger, one addressed often.

History and Historical Figures in the Changes

This book is associated with the foundation of the Zhou dynasty around 1045 BCE, and with the events that occurred in the generation just before the conquest and the one after it. It assumes a knowledge of the stories that surround this great change. While modern scholars are still arguing about the timing and nature of these events, few doubt that they occurred. The following summary is intended to convey the truth as seen by most of those who created and used this book and other classics during the Zhou dynasty.[7]

The Shang kings had ruled China for many centuries. While the first Shang king had been a good man, the last was not. He

---

5. See Chang in *Cambridge History of Ancient China.*

6. See *Shijing* 258.

7. For more recent views of the same events, see Li Feng and *Cambridge History of Ancient China*, inter alia.

was selfish, cruel, and unpredictable. (Archaeological evidence suggests that he may have suffered from lead poisoning, since he drank strong ale heated in bronze vessels.) Some of his advisors tried to change his policies by remonstrating with him. Instead of listening, he killed some of them and imprisoned others. Many of these courageous critics are remembered by name in the histories and poems. One of them was the man later known as King Wen. Although he served at the Shang court, he came of the Zhou people. He was very wise and very timely. Although he was a better man than the last Shang king, he tried to give the king good advice. When this proved impossible, and he was thrown into prison, he used his time there to organize existing textual fragments into what is now know as the *Zhou (Book of) Changes.*

Thus he is one of those who fashioned this text bearing good advice throughout the ages, for those who will hear.

Before he was imprisoned, Wen ruled the Zhou people well. His consideration for others was exemplified by the way he treated his royal bride when she arrived from an allied state. Instead of awaiting her in his walled city, Wen went to her before she arrived, thereby expressing his honor for her.[8] Their son, later called Wu, built up the strength of the Zhou people and waited until they had the cohesion necessary for a successful conquest of Shang. In a decisive battle, the weaker Zhou army defeated the far more numerous but by then disheartened Shang troops. (Scholars disagree about the date, but not about the reality of the conflict and conquest.) King Wu then moved Shang royalty away from their traditional seat of power, but permitted them to continue their religious and other rituals. He avoided mass slaughter and did his best to serve the interests of all the people of both Shang and Zhou. He set up a feudal system based on

---

8.   See *Shijing* 236 (Da ming) and *Ch'un Ch'iu,* Hsien, 15th year, 2 (James Legge, *Chinese Classics,* vol. V (Hong Kong: Hong Kong University Press, 1960), pages 467–469.

his family. He did not try to rule all of China directly, but kept only a small territory to support himself and his descendents. The rest he entrusted to his relatives and followers, to rule as they saw fit. The dynasty he established lasted for nearly eight hundred years. He kept many Shang customs, but drank less and behaved more responsibly. He honored his father by giving him the posthumous name and title King Wen, so that he would not outrank his father.

This was a patriarchal world, but it had matriarchal elements. Some Shang queens ruled their own walled cities. One led several successful military campaigns. Elite women had far more power than male peasants. All women had natural feet. (The custom of binding feet began nearly two thousand years later and took centuries to become widespread.) At the beginning of this period, men and women were probably about the same height, but by the end of the Zhou, most men were taller than most women, due to dietary changes.[9]

Religious Context

The Zhou world which we see in the *Changes* was a deeply religious one, with seasonal and religio-political rituals simlar to those of the preceding Shang dynasty. These events included sacrifices of animals and strong drink to ancestor and nature spirits, and, most importantly, to a deity associated with the Sky, *Tian* (traditionally translated as Heaven, though it never refers to a place where good people go after death).

The Shang used this term as well as Lord on High (*Shangdi*), and the Zhou did as well. There is no abrupt switch from one term

---

9. Ekaterina Pechenkina, "Life in Early Farming Communities of Northern China: A Bioarchaeological Account," unpublished paper presented April 10, 2010, to University Seminar on Early China, Columbia University. For more information on Professor Pechenkina's research, see her website at Queens College, City University of New York.

to the other, though Zhou texts refer to the Sky (*Tian*) far more often than Shang did.

Theological speculation does not seem to have been a concern of these people, for the Classics do not define the Sky entity. However, they assume that this Being was above all beings and things and cared for the people as a whole, to the extent that *Tian* sanctioned the replacement of the irresponsible Shang ruling family by the trustworthy Zhou. However, *Tian* is not a personal god, has no anthropomorphic features, and rarely performs miracles. Neither *Tian* nor *Shangdi* spoke in words written on stone or spoken to prophets. This is a major reason for the strength of the oracular tradition in early China.

Societal Structure

Class structure and hierarchy were essential to Zhou society and governance. The elite ruling class was small, probably a tenth of the population or less, though we have no census data for this early period. This class was itself stratified into ranks of ruling families and higher and lower nobility. The elite possessed land and the peasants attached to it in fiefs which produced income in the forms of grain, cloth, and labor service. The elite also were among the few with literacy and political influence. The vast majority of the populace were peasants in nuclear families where most men farmed the land and most women raised silkworms, wove cloth, made clothes and shoes, and prepared food.

The primary political unit was the walled city, where the highest nobles lived and ruled. During the Shang, some walled cities were governed by queens. Archaeological studies of cities reflect a stratified society, with separate areas for markets and for artisans specializing in making bronze vessels and implements, pottery, and other tools. The cities were walled because warfare was still common, a fact reflected in many of the *Changes'* hexagrams. Outside the walls was an area where more people lived and raised crops for the city. In times of strife, these people probably fled inside the walls for protection. Population density may have thinned farther from the cities, and boundaries between dukedoms and fiefs may have been ill-defined.

Women's roles varied. We have little information on peasants. However both recent archaeological finds and ancient texts provide us with information on some elite women. At least one Shang queen governed and led military campaigns with significant autonomy, as her husband's second in command.[10] While most institutions were patriarchal, royal and noble women outranked many men. Mothers of rulers were due the deference of their ruling sons. Rulers might have multiple wives and more lesser women, but their wives were often of equally distinguished royal lineages. Elite marriages were arranged to solidify alliances between states, with the hope that a grandchild shared by two states would be unlikely to attack his mother's home. In at least one case, when a Zhou king sent his wife home and replaced her with a woman of lower rank, the former queen's father invaded his territory. On the second try, this invasion was successful.

No women had bound feet in this era. That was thousands of years in the future. Women could and did remarry. This was not a society which valued equality. Hierarchy was assumed to be the norm in all realms. But with multiple types of hierarchy, rank and age usually outweighed gender.

Our understanding of the status of women in early China has changed dramatically since the 1920s, and is still evolving rapidly. There are many controversies among respected scholars in the field. But archaeological and textual evidence clearly show that some elite women used the *Changes*. And most scholars would agree that

---

10. See Elizabeth Childs-Johnson, "FuZi the Shang Woman Warrior," in the *Biographical Dictionary of Chinese Women, vol. I, Antiquity through Sui (1600 BCE–618 CE)*, edited by Lily Xiao Hong Lee and A.D. Stefanowska. Chinese University of Hong Kong Libraries Publication, 2007, pp. 19–25.

Chinese elite women lost rights and freedoms over the centuries.

This is a very brief and general summary of a long and highly complex period of history. Major discoveries and analytic break-throughs continue with remarkable rapidity.[11] Furthermore, I agree with Richard John Lynn (1994, p. 8) that

> ...there is no one single Classic of Changes but rather as many versions of it as there are different commentaries on it. The text of the classic is so dense and so opaque in so many places that its meaning depends entirely on how any particular commentary interprets it. Some interpretations, especially those of Cheng Yi and Zhu Xi, have become standard and orthodox, but the authority they carry, it seems to me, was derived not from any so-called perfect reading of the text but from the fact that the Cheng-Zhu version of Neo-Confucianism became the cultural and intellectual orthodoxy of traditional China; thus their commentaries, including those on the Changes, had to be correct. My approach to the Changes is entirely different. The commentary of Wang Bi is the historical product of a certain time and place.... a product that can tell us much about the development of Chinese intellectual thought.... should reveal how much variety and vitality traditional Chinese thought could achieve.

I have tried to summarize some of the most important aspects of the eras that gave birth to the core of the *Changes*, because I believe that understanding the historical context of a book helps us to understand its meaning. However, I do not claim complete knowledge of all the new scholarship on Shang and Zhou dynasties. I provide some Further Reading for readers eager to learn more. And I have

---

11. For example, since I began this work, another early form of the text has been found and is being analyzed. While it may differ little from other versions, those differences may be significant, but they are beyond the scope of this work.

dared to share the insights gained through thirty years of teaching Chinese history and introducing my students to the *Changes*, with the hope that the conversations that have clustered around this difficult but highly evocative text will continue, and include more women and men within and outside the fields of China studies.

About the Translation

In my acknowledgements of the many scholars whose work has laid the foundations for mine, I have provided more information on my translation and interpretive methods.

Although I began this work in 1997, with research into a less anachronistic reading of hexagram 44, I worked through most of the other 63 hexagrams during my 2004–2005 sabbatical year at Cambridge University. The Needham Research Institute provided an office where I worked on a biography of Zhang Heng, a scholar, official, and scientist who also consulted the *Yijing*. Each morning, I began the day (and my first cup of coffee) at the table in my flat, looking out over the fields west of Cambridge. Here I wrote out the Chinese text of each *Zhouyi* hexagram and its image, as well as the characters in the Mawangdui version of the text. I used several dictionaries and consulted four very different translations. I wrote down possible English meanings, then worked towards sentences, between the lines of Chinese text. I soon realized that if I wrote scholarly notes justifying every choice of character or English word that the task would take not months or years, but decades. I used the findings of others, particularly the recently published (and annotated) translations of Ed Shaughnessy and Richard Lynn. The first provides a brief overview of the main differences between the received and Mawangdui texts and tries to do without later commentaries, as I do. The Lynn work provides a complete translation of the entire *Zhouyi* and all of Wang Bi's commentary, carefully distinguishes between text, commentary, and translators assumptions, and provides a wealth of material gleaned from other commentaries, both early and late. The reader interested in these details should look at these works and their notes, and I have tried to make it easy for you to do so by putting the relevant page numbers at the foot of each hexagram's discussion.

I also used the resources of the Needham Research Institute (scholars as well as books) and Cambridge's University Library to pursue particularly difficult points. I shared drafts of hexagrams with a seminar at Clare Hall Cambridge and with people who have consulted this version of the *Changes* over the years. There were revisions at each stage, and the current version owes much to the editorial advice of Sandra Korinchak, Michael Ochs, and Anne Hockenos.

Every translator is faced with a maddening array of compulsory choices if she is to attempt an entire text, as I have. In general, I have followed the following principles: I have tried to reflect the fact that readers have included women as well as men by making pronouns gender neutral. I have sought consistency in translation; that is, I have tried to use the same translation for the same phrases throughout. When I was faced with two very different possible meanings, I have looked at the hexagram as a whole and chosen what seemed to me to be the most consistent alternative. Thus one reason I believe hexagram 44 refers to a royal marriage is that several of the lines use figures of speech which were common fertility images at the time, in a work of nearly equal antiquity, the Book of Songs.[12] Similarly, segments of bamboo seemed more

---

12. I am grateful to Michael Nylan for pointing these out and to Fongyee Walker for verifying this and other *Shijing* metaphors' meanings.

related to branching and the other lines of the hexagram referred to in the received version as "work on what is spoiled."

Why did I include the images, when I know that they were composed later than the *Zhouyi* proper? I find this segment of the *Changes* similar in feeling to the *Zhouyi* in that they contain few references to cosmic principles like *yin* and *yang*. And I have lived with these words for many years, writing down the characters in the morning and carrying them throughout the day, memorizing them, and writing the characters over and over when I could, usually during meetings when I needed to say as little as possible. Because they have "spoken" to me, I have provided my thoughts on how the trigrams, situations, and ethical acts endorsed in them may be related.

Conventions Used by This Translation

Most subjects and pronouns: the subjects of many sentences are unstated, and the original text's pronoun usually used to refer back to these implicit subjects is vaguer than any one English term, since it can mean: *he, she, it, they, them, her, him,* etc. There are other times when the same word means *of* in classical Chinese. Other translations usually use *he* or *him,* since many, if not most, early readers of the *Changes* were men. Also, "man," "he," was at one time accepted philosophical usage meaning "one human being." This is no longer the case. The most accurate translation would be "s/he/it," but that is awkward. For a time I considered using *she* throughout, since it seemed reasonable for one translation out of the many to recognize women readers. However, when I used the text to do readings for men, I found myself changing this to "you" or "he" as I went along.

Although, strictly speaking, "you" is inaccurate, since another word is used for this, it appears fairly rarely in the Zhou *Changes,* and is one of the few gender neutral pronouns denoting people in English. Generally speaking, I have used "you."

Verbs: In many languages, verbs have tenses and are conjugated. This makes them easy to differentiate from other parts of speech. In Chinese, they are not conjugated and the tense is often unclear. In other texts, this problem is minimized by sentence patterns that place time words, like *tomorrow*, first. In this text, this is rarely the case. Yet English forced me to decide whether to treat a word as a noun or a verb, and to select a verb tense. To some extent, this was a rather artificial enterprise, since such clear distinctions are not in the original text. I have tried to maintain fairly consistent verb tenses throughout, but I encourage the reader to change the tense and see whether that seems to change the meaning for them in the situation they are considering. If it does, it may be wise to write down what the difference seems to be, so that you can reflect on that later, as you consult a trusted advisor. Using the text in doing readings for others I often found that the future tense seemed appropriate since we were considering the probable results of a given decision or action, even though it is not clearly indicated in specific words in the text.

You should: 君子 **Junzi** (chūn-tzu): While this is too nuanced a term for an easy one-word translation, I needed one or two words to represent it. Others translate it as *gentleman* or *superior man*. I have chosen "you should" for the following reasons: There is general agreement that the word refers to the best kind of person, one worthy of being chosen as the heir to the throne (literally, it means *the lord's son*). (For much of the Zhou period, rulers had many sons, and one of the sons of a royal wife was chosen, not always the eldest. This led to rivalry and deaths, but it meant that cruel or incompetent sons could be passed over.) For a time I considered trying to find a gender neutral or feminine equivalent of "a prince of a fellow," but modern usage of "princess" is far from the ethical paragon I sought.

This term is used in most images *(xiang)*. When it is replaced, the alternative usually means *ruler*. I believe it refers to a person worthy of great responsibility, authority, and leadership. Perhaps "you at your responsible best" would do, but this is quite awkward in sentences. Usually this word appears in combination with a verb or verbs describing the kinds of action this best-of-all-people should do under these circumstances. In other words, references to *junzi* are a form of moral exhortation in many Zhou texts. For this reason, I have used "you should," which is consistent with the pronoun usage described above.

In some cases, usually one of the lines in the *Zhouyi* itself, "you should" seemed inappropriate, and I have used "one worthy of power" instead, since that particular context seemed to call for that wording.

Queen (or Ruler): Hou: *Hou* can mean either *after* or *a ruler*. For most of imperial Chinese history, it meant an empress. For Zhou, since there were no emperors yet, I have used "queen" in the one place where this appears, in the image of hexagram 44. This is, I believe, more accurate than the commonly used "prince, he," and fits with many aspects of that hexagram. (See it and my article on the same.) Liu has 后 as the original character.

Recurring Terms

Cross the great water. Literal meaning: cross the Yellow River, the main river in the North China plain. Meaning: make a major move or change. Often described as likely to be effective (literally, *profitable*) or not.

Great (or supreme) success. The word for *great* represents a natural spring of water rather than mere size. To me this suggests a success which is as sure and ongoing as a long-lived natural spring. What success consists of is a complex issue, one not defined very clearly in the original text.

King Wen is very closely associated with the formation of this text, as is the dynasty which his son founded. For information on his life, see "Understanding the Context of the *Book of Changes*." In this text, he appears as a moral exemplar, a wise and competent nobleman who made the most effective use of whatever situation he was in. Before his marriage to the princess who begat the conqueror of Shang, he built a bridge of boats in order to go to her and make her progress to her new home easier (Book of Songs, #236). He served the Shang king of his own time with loyal criticism of bad policies (remonstrance), and accepted the resulting imprisonment. While he was in prison, he used his time well, and is credited with bringing order to the fragments which became the Zhou *Changes* at that time. Confucius and his followers venerated Wen, as did his son, who conferred the posthumous title of King.

Misfortune. The character shows a box with an X in it.

No blame. Could also mean no trouble or no distress. Since other words also mean trouble, and I did not wish to repeat every possibility every time, I chose this one alternative, as what seems more likely to me. However, trouble or distress are almost equally valid.

Persisting is effective. A frequently recurring term in this prognostication text, which could also mean "consulting the oracle is appropriate," since on Shang oracle bones, it seems to mean *to divine*. However, in hexagram 2, we read that a mare does this. I find it hard to imagine a horse manipulating yarrow stalks with its hooves or making a turtle shell crack. Wilhelm/Baynes has "perseverance furthers." Actually, the two meanings, apparently opposed in English, are rather close when we understand how the *Changes* were used. Generally speaking, the person contemplating an action did all the usual things a person does when faced with an important decision: gather information, assess preparedness, confer with colleagues to see whether or not they are of like mind and might support the intended action. After reaching a nearly final decision, inquirers posed a question basically stating what they planned, and when they planned to do it. They then consulted the oracle as a method of verifying the correctness of both action and timing. Afterwards, they usually consulted experts for an objective interpretation and guidance. Thus divination is part of a final stage of decision making, and taking the proposed action and persevering in that direction seems to be related to the wisdom of doing the divining.

Either interpretation is valid. Given the mare, I've used "persist" or "persevere" throughout.

Remorse disappears. Or regrets vanish.

See the great person. To consult with someone of greater wisdom, knowledge, or authority. Frequently recommended to even the most powerful and wisest of people, such as good kings.

How to Use
the Book of Changes

The material in the *Book of Changes* existed long before it was collected into a book, and the order of the six-line figures or hexagrams has varied. For this reason, starting on page one and reading straight through is not the best way to use the book. Also, it is not the way most Chinese have used it for centuries. It is better to dip into it, read a short section, and come back to it later.

In structure, the book has 64 sections, each associated with a hexagram of solid and broken lines. Why are there 64 total? Because if you have six-line figures, and each line can be solid or broken, there are sixty-four possible combinations.

Each hexagram is made up of two trigrams. These trigrams are of great antiquity and have been used to represent natural objects in China for thousands of years. They are so old that their origins are quite obscure.[13] Some are clearly related to early forms of characters. For example, *water* looks like the ancient character for water, tipped on its side. As you can see, each pair below is the inverse of the other: sky (that is, all above earth) is the opposite of earth, water the opposite of fire, lake the opposite of mountain, thunder of wind.

---

13. For more information on their meanings in the *I Ching*, see Joseph Needham, *Science and Civilization in China,* vol. II, pp. 313–314.

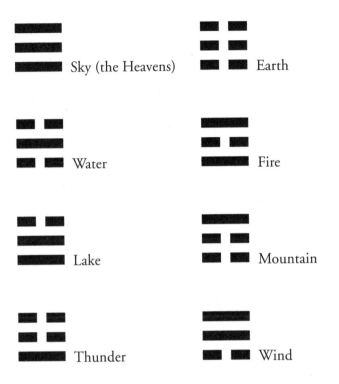

Sky (the Heavens)

Earth

Water

Fire

Lake

Mountain

Thunder

Wind

When these eight are combined, 64 six-line figures (hexagrams) are generated. These are the sections of the *Book of Changes*.

The Image: A Situation, and Stages within It

Each hexagram represents a human situation considered analogous to a natural object and situation. The text of the book, which appears as several lines directly below the heading containing the number and name of the hexagram, offers a description of the situation as a whole, as does the "Image" text further below. My comments on the image follow, and also relate to the hexagram as a whole.

The numbered lines ("Six in the first place," "Nine in the second place," and so on), which are read starting at the bottom of the hexagram, may represent stages within this situation.[14]

For example, in hexagram 1, we are reading about stages in the life of a truly great person, one worthy of leading all the people and of founding a new and better order. (In East Asia, this kind of person was associated with a dragon, since dragons appeared only in the presence of the best kind of leader.)

In the first numbered line of hexagram 1, it is considered unsafe even for great persons to reveal themselves. In the third line, a good person has risen to an appropriate position of responsibility but finds it impossible to get everything done on time despite working hard all day. In the fifth line, the leader has reached the apogee of success, and is reminded that even the greatest needs good advice. The sixth line provides a salutary warning against arrogance.

While ideal situations are described in the *Changes,* by its very nature, the book recognizes that the ethical actions of a good person must fit a given situation. As the book says itself: "Great is the power of timely action."

Ways to Use the Changes

- **Thematic method**: Some people find it useful to read two or three hexagrams on a similar topic, such as progress, being new in town, or feeling stuck.

  For example, if you are feeling lonely, you might benefit from reading about the Wanderer in hexagram 56 or Sprouting in hexagram 3. If you feel stuck, you might look at hexagrams 3, 5, 12, and 60, or others with the same theme. If you are

---

14. There are four numeric possible results from tossing three coins: 6, 7, 8, and 9. Sevens and eights are more likely, as they represent two of one side and one of the other, which is more probable than three of a kind. Sixes and nines, since they are less likely, were believed to be more significant. These are the only lines which are considered to be in the process of change, the subject of the book. And they are the only lines on which there are comments.

interested in Chinese attitudes toward major political change, you would want to study hexagram 49.

- **Temple usage:** Many Asians consult the *Changes* when visiting a Buddhist or Daoist (Taoist) temple. There they shake a container holding sixty-four wooden or bamboo strips, one for each hexagram, until one drops out. The temple attendant then hands them a piece of paper with the text of the hexagram, and may be asked to interpret it for them.

- **Consulting the text:** To consult the *Changes* for guidance, in the most traditional method, people with questions sorted and resorted fifty milfoil stalks six times in a complex process that yielded six numbers between 6 and 9. Later, similar results were obtained using coins, the method familiar to Westerners. This method is described in detail in the next section, together with two examples. (Chinese coins were inscribed on one side only; we will substitute coins with heads and tails, considering heads as the inscribed side, as do Lynn and Wilhelm.)

How to Consult the Text

The following guidelines are based on examples of divination in the *Tso chuan* and on three decades of teaching the text. I believe that following these principles is more likely to produce a meaningful result. However, I realize that readers may not always have time to do every step. Sometimes simply asking "What should I think about today?" is all I can manage. You will find your own way.

1. Formulate a question about an action you plan to take or not take. The question must include a time span and must not be made up of multiple parts. It must also be

about you, rather than another person. Examples: Should I change jobs this year? How directly should I express my love tomorrow when I see the person I'm attracted to? As I think about my summer plans this month, what image from the *Changes* would be most helpful for me to meditate on?

Then take the following steps.

2. Write the question at the top of a sheet of paper and write the numbers from 6 to 1 on six separate lines:

6)
5)
4)
3)
2)
1)

3. Read your question—aloud, if possible—while shaking three coins in your hands. Drop the coins and record the number of heads and tails next to the number 1. Example:

1) 2 heads   +   1 tail

4. Repeat the procedure five more times, restating your question each time. Let's say your list now looks like this:

6)   1 head   +   2 tails
5)   2 heads   +   1 tail
4)   3 heads   +   0 tails
3)   1 head   +   2 tails
2)   0 heads   +   3 tails
1)   2 heads   +   1 tail

5. Counting heads as 2 and tails as 3, cal-
    culate a number for each of the six sets
    as follows:

REMINDER	
Head	= 2
Tail	= 3

1 head   +   2 tails   =   **8**
(1×2) + (2×3) =   *8*

2 heads   +   1 tail   =   **7**
(2×2) + (1×3) =   *7*

3 heads   +   0 tails   =   **6**
(3×2) + (0×3) =   *6*

1 head   +   2 tails   =   **8**
(1×2) + (2×3) =   *8*

0 heads   +   3 tails   =   **9**
(0×2) + (3×3) =   *9*

2 heads   +   1 tail   =   **7**
(2×2) + (1×3) =   *7*

Your list would now look like this:

6) 1 head   +   2 tails   =   8
5) 2 heads   +   1 tail   =   7
4) 3 heads   +   0 tails   =   6
3) 1 head   +   2 tails   =   8
2) 0 heads   +   3 tails   =   9
1) 2 heads   +   1 tail   =   7

6. Convert these numbers to the lines they represent in the hexagrams in the *Book of Changes,* as follows: 6 and 8 are broken lines, 7 and 9 are solid lines. The resulting lines form a hexagram:

REMINDER	
6	= broken
7	= solid
8	= broken
9	= solid

6)	1 head	+ 2 tails	=	8	▬▬ ▬▬
5)	2 heads	+ 1 tail	=	7	▬▬▬▬▬
4)	3 heads	+ 0 tails	=	6	▬▬X▬▬
3)	1 head	+ 2 tails	=	8	▬▬ ▬▬
2)	3 tails	+ 0 heads	=	9	▬▬◉▬▬
1)	2 heads	+ 1 tail	=	7	▬▬▬▬▬

7. Now apply the following changes to form a second hexagram:

REMINDER	
6: broken & changing	▬x▬ → ▬▬▬
7: solid	▬▬▬ → ▬ ▬
8: broken	▬ ▬ → ▬ ▬
9: solid & changing	▬●▬ → ▬ ▬

6 is a broken line so weak that it can change only by becoming strong (solid);

7 is a solid line that is stable and will remain unchanged (solid);

8 is a broken line that is also stable and will remain unchanged (broken);

9 is a solid line so strong that it can change only by becoming weak (broken).

					1st hexagram		2nd hexagram
					↓		↓
6)	1 head	+ 2 tails	=	8	▬▬ ▬▬	*still*	▬▬ ▬▬
5)	2 heads	+ 1 tail	=	7	▬▬▬▬▬	*still*	▬▬▬▬▬
4)	3 heads	+ 0 tails	=	6	▬▬X▬▬	*then*	▬▬▬▬▬

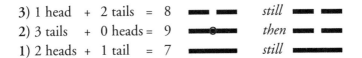

3) 1 head + 2 tails = 8   ━━ ━━   *still* ━━ ━━
2) 3 tails + 0 heads = 9   ━━●━━   *then* ━━ ━━
1) 2 heads + 1 tail   = 7   ━━━━   *still* ━━━━

The first hexagram will yield the immediate result of your planned action; the second hexagram will yield future results of the action.

8. In the chart on the next pages, find the column that matches the upper trigram (top half) of your first hexagram, then find the row that matches the lower trigram. You will find your hexagram and its number at the juncture of that column and row. Repeat to find your second hexagram and its number.

   In our example, the first hexagram is number 60. (The upper trigram is WATER, and the lower trigram is LAKE; these meet in the chart at hexagram 60.)

   In our example, the second hexagram is number 17. (The upper trigram is LAKE, and the lower trigram is THUNDER; these meet in the chart at hexagram 17.)

9. Copy down the name and brief description (see the list in the table of contents) of each of your hexagrams. Jot down your first, instinctive reaction, whatever it may be, for use later on.

   Then, turn to the text of your hexagram. For each 6 and 9 that you have (refer back to your findings in Step 7), reread your question and read any numbered-line comment that appears in the hexagram, such as "Nine in the third place…" These comments, which may indicate danger or effectiveness, are the most focused responses to your question.

   Write down both the comment and your first response to it. If it makes no sense to you, add a question mark.

Lower trigram \ Upper trigram	天 Sky	雷 Thunder	水 Water
天 Sky	01	34	05
雷 Thunder	25	51	03
水 Water	06	40	29
山 Mountain	33	62	39
地 Earth	12	16	08
風 Wind	44	32	48
火 Fire	13	55	63
澤 Lake	10	54	60

Since this translation aims for clarity and simplicity, and focuses on the meanings of the image for each hexagram, the trigram names shown here include the characters for

山 Mountain	地 Earth	風 Wind	火 Fire	澤 Lake
26	11	09	14	43
27	24	42	21	17
04	07	59	64	47
52	15	53	56	31
23	02	20	35	45
18	46	57	50	28
22	36	37	30	49
41	19	61	38	58

the meanings of the trigrams. The older names and characters for the trigrams, some of them obscure, are not shown.

Read only the remarks relating to *your* 6's and 9's, as these are the only ones that apply to you at this time. Then write down your honest feelings about the different possibilities for danger, effectiveness, or confusion.

Finally, read the image of your hexagram, as well as the commentary that follows.

10. Now find the text for your second hexagram, which may represent the future results of what you planned to do in your question. For this hexagram, read only the text (the lines immediately after the page's main heading) and the image, as well as my comments on the image. (Because your lines have stopped changing, they are no longer 6's or 9's, so do not read any of the six numbered lines.)

Reading the Images

After the text and the six numbered lines is a description of the hexagram's image. Each trigram represents a natural object, and the image describes a natural phenomenon in which one element is above another, for example, fire below a mountain. This is coupled with a description of the ethical actions most suited to the situation described by this hexagram. The original text states what a *junzi,* or ideal person—really any ethical person—would do. In this book, instead of "an ideal person would …," the phrase "you should …" is used.

My thoughts on the relationship between the natural image and the moral exhortation appear below the translated image text. These comments are based on early Chinese history and thought and are intended to help you discern your own meaning from the most important allusions to aspects of early Chinese culture. They are my own efforts to find meaning and they often differ from past commentaries or opinions. If these words speak to you, write them down as well. Then take the time to write as many of your own responses as you can to what you have read.

Frequently, the meaning and situation will still seem confused. Your situation and question are probably complex and troubling, or you would not have asked. Keep in mind that the *Book of Changes* was designed for people living in a very different time, though many of their concerns remain ours as well. Focus on any words or phrases that seem significant to you. Write down your feelings about this process, or about how the situation you are thinking about looks to you now. Don't be surprised if the same people or problems start to look different.

Now put this all aside and return to your normal life. Then, just before going to sleep, read through your question and the responses, as well as your first thoughts. Try to see one of the natural images clearly in your mind as you meditate on it or as you drift off to sleep. In the morning, find a quiet space and once again read through what you wrote. You may find that the words in the *Changes* have different meanings from those of the day before and that you perceive your situation differently. Again write as much as you can about your question and the responses elicited by this process. You may want to consult a trusted counselor or friend about what it all may mean. This process may help you see aspects of a situation that you had ignored but that are crucial to a successful outcome.

You may find it useful to come back to these words and images over the next few days. Look at any change in the meaning of the words and what your changing perceptions may reveal about the way you see the situation. Again, use the images as meditation subjects for the period you planned to do so. Expect to find wisdom though not clarity. If the answer seems clear, be sure to read all sections again, carefully. An unmitigatedly positive answer is very rare. The text is, by its nature, notoriously difficult to interpret.

There are many historical examples of people who rushed to do what they wished, thinking the oracle supported this. They often went astray.

For really difficult decisions, people in the past also consulted oracles by using turtle shells. Rulers and leaders who used oracles knew they were unclear and understood that they needed the help of others to make wise decisions, so they usually asked for advice about both the oracles and their decisions. It's a good idea to get advice from someone you consider wise or a good listener, the kind of person referred to as a great person in the *Changes*. Of course you should never make a major decision based on what any one person says or what you find in any one book, and you should certainly not do something you know is wrong just because you think the *Changes* says it's alright. (Chinese history has many examples of the havoc this can create. For example, a duke, smitten by the beautiful bride he had brought for his son, wanted to take her for himself. One oracle seemed to condone this, and the other did not. His advisor wisely warned against cheating his son in this way. The duke did what he wanted—he took the bride—and he and his state suffered. See *Tso Chuan*, tr. Burton Watson, for more detail about this episode.)

Generally speaking, the book encourages us to be responsible, kind, and thoughtful in deciding what we should do. In some situations, prompt action is wise. In others, the best we can do is watch, survive, and try to learn from what we see. Often what looks like a terrible situation has hidden advantages and what appears to be a great situation has hidden dangers.

Using the book may enable you to see aspects of a difficult situation that you have failed to notice, may remind you that nothing lasts forever, or may not seem to relate to your concern at all. But the natural images associated with human situations have a special beauty all their own. The people who created the book believed that we can learn from watching nature and its changes. They were startled, as we are, by thunder and lightning, but they were also encouraged, for they recognized them as signs of the rain they needed.

If this book encourages you to walk outdoors, really see the natural objects around you, and adopt nature as one of your teachers, it will have served part of its purpose. Scientists have shown that both the walking and the focus on trees and grass help heal our feelings by encouraging the release of endorphins. Even if you cannot walk outside, this version of the *Changes* can bring you vivid images of nature: storms and calm, dissolution and persistence. It can speak to you, as it has to Confucius, Jung, and many others over the centuries. At the very least, it will remind you that thousands of others have wondered what to do and tried to do what was both right and kind. They did not always succeed, but through the book and the thoughts that continue to cluster around it, we speak to each other and remember our common humanity, fears, and joys.

Following are two examples of the process explained above.

Example #1, Inquiry with Responses
(This happens to be an example with no changing lines.)

Situation: I have worked so hard in my new career, but I feel I have made very little progress, and I am exhausted.

(Step 1: Formulate a question.)

Question: Should I give up on this position now, and move to something else?

(Steps 2, 3, 4, 5, and 6 result in this hexagram. By following Step 7, you see that this hexagram has no changing lines; so there is no separate, second hexagram in this case.)

```
6)  8   ▬▬  ▬▬
5)  7   ▬▬▬▬▬
4)  8   ▬▬  ▬▬
3)  8   ▬▬  ▬▬
2)  8   ▬▬  ▬▬
1)  7   ▬▬▬▬▬
```

(Step 8 tells you that the relevant hexagram is number 3.)

(Step 9 is to read and consider the text. One part of Step 9—for each 6 and 9 you have, read the relevant numbered lines—doesn't apply here, because you had no 6's or 9's. You had only 7's and 8's. So, focus on the hexagram's text and image, then the commentary, noting down your thoughts.)

3   Sprouting

Sprouting ensures continuing growth. Persistence is effective; don't start a journey now. It is good to delegate responsibilities to those you trust.

(Your comment:) Sounds like it's not time to move.

Image

Clouds and thunder: the image of sprouting. You should set strong warp strings to the loom.

Thunder scares me. So does being a beginner here. But maybe I am sort of like a new sprout right now, and feeling weak and tired is just a stage. How are looms strung? How can thunder, a sprout, and some loom threads relate to me?

(Reading the commentary:)

Clouds and thunder were welcome signs on the north China plains, where rainfall was scarce and too much sun could spell death for crops and people. Although the clouds darken the light for a time, and the thunder may be frightening, they usually signal the arrival of the rain necessary for growing things. Similarly, stringing a loom with the long warp threads which will provide strength to a fabric is a difficult process, requiring more than one person to accomplish it. This is a time of new growth and of setting the stage for further growth. This stage usually includes difficulties, but surmounting them will result in a framework, an environment, which will support sustained growth and productivity.

The character that names this hexagram depicts a sprout, a seedling at the stage when, after developing its roots, it has just managed to pierce the crust of the earth and push its first tendril above ground. Many of us can remember a childhood experience of watching a bean go through this process in a clear container, so that we could see the roots developing within the earth. What is visible above ground looks fairly pathetic....

Well, the exhaustion is real, but if it's just a stage, maybe it's not so bad. I remember growing a lima bean in second grade. It took forever to grow roots and it looked really puny and pale when it finally got one sprout above ground. But after that, it turned green and did fine.

A secondary aspect of this stage is delegation. The Zhou kings, who consulted the forerunner of the *Book of Changes*, reigned for nearly eight hundred years but they never tried to rule their entire kingdom directly....

The lines of the hexagram make it clear that we are not expected to go it alone. Even the greatest person, with the most developed wisdom and self-control, cannot succeed without guides, just as a ruler going hunting requires expert assistance for a successful hunt. If trustworthy help is not available, it is usually better to postpone attempts to move ahead. However, if someone is so committed to us that they have stood by us for ten years, without a commitment on our side, then they are not thieves but truly sincere about spending their lives with us. We need this kind of ally, but we also need to avoid people who might rob us.

Who could help me now? Has anyone offered me help? If accepting their help is a strength, maybe I should welcome their advice instead of taking it as an insult.

Example #2, Inquiry with Responses

(This is an example with one changing line.)

Situation: I know I am qualified for my job advising the leader of my country, and that he really trusts me. But there is so much nasty political infighting, and so many people and policies are wrong.

(Step 1: Formulate a question.)

Question: Should I retire now?

(Steps 2, 3, 4, 5, and 6 result in the below "first" hexagram. Step 7 results in the below "second" hexagram.)

		first	second
6)	9	▬▬◉▬▬	▬▬ ▬▬
5)	7	▬▬▬▬▬	▬▬▬▬▬
4)	7	▬▬▬▬▬	▬▬▬▬▬
3)	7	▬▬▬▬▬	▬▬▬▬▬
2)	8	▬▬ ▬▬	▬▬ ▬▬
1)	8	▬▬ ▬▬	▬▬ ▬▬

(Step 8 tells you that the relevant hexagrams are numbers 33 [first] and 31 [second]. Read the first hexagram's text, relevant lines, and image, then the commentary, noting down your thoughts.)

33 Retreat

Retreat. In minor matters, persistence is effective.

(Your comment:) Sounds like retreat might be the successful route this time. Odd.

(Step 9: You have "Nine in the sixth place," so read that numbered line.)

Nine at the top: Flying retreat: it all works. [lit., there is nothing without benefit]

This is the most direct response, and it seems pretty clear: getting out now is definitely the right move.

Image

Beneath the sky, there is a mountain: the image of retreat. You should keep shallow people at a distance, not with hatred but with reserve.

Well, I don't mind being told I'm as great as a mountain, especially when I feel other people hate me. Retiring might be the right thing to do. But I guess I'd better not say all those nasty things I'd like to. I'm leaving now, but I don't know the future. I guess I'd better just say as little as possible and leave quietly, even if I am in the right.

(Reading the commentary:)
Mountains are great, towering over surrounding lands, even though they cannot reach the sky. Similarly, even the greatest and best people cannot expect a life of continuous progress. For each

of us, there are times when we must retreat in the face of stronger forces and distance ourselves from shallow souls....

(Step 10: Now consider your second hexagram, which may represent the future results.)

31 Reciprocity, Respect

Mutual respect: success. Persistence is effective. To take this woman brings good fortune.

> *Resigning this top position will lead to success and mutual respect? That's not what most people think. But the kind of people I admire might actually react that way, once I'm out of here. Maybe it's not a dead end at all.*

Image

Above the mountain, a lake: the image of reciprocity/respect. You should receive others with emptiness. [That is, truly hear them.]

> *Refreshing water at the top of a mountain: that's really different from being beset by people wanting me to help them get ahead. Being retired and among real friends might be a very pleasant change from this position. Certainly there would be less pressure.*

(Reading the commentary:)
Lakes rarely lie high in the mountains, much less above them. Yet when we find pure water at high elevations, we welcome it and are refreshed. Rain or a spring has found a hollow in which to collect.

In order to be truly receptive to others, we need to empty ourselves of expectations and our own ways of seeing, lest they prevent our accurate hearing....

Historical note: China's greatest early scientist, an advisor to two rulers, Zhang Heng (78–139), received this response when he consulted the *Changes* around 133.[15] Zhang Heng did leave this post. Soon afterwards, he served capably as the governor of a province. Finally, he was given another high position in the central government. He wrote superb poetry which is still read today. A reconstruction of his earthquake sensor has a prominent position in the historical museum in Beijing.

---

15. He documented his feelings about his situation and the response of the *Changes* in a long poem, *Rhapsody on Contemplating the Mystery.* For a translation, see Xiao Tong, *Wen Xuan,* translated and annotated by David R. Knechtges (Princeton University Press, 1996), vol. 3, pp. 104–139.

The Original I Ching

乾 ䷀

1

(qián) The Creative

The creative. Success flows. Persistence is effective.

- **Nine in the first place:** The hidden dragon. Don't do it*!*
  Even if you were perfect, this would be the wrong time to take the action you are considering.

- **Nine in the second place:** Meeting a dragon in a field. Seek the advice of someone wiser than you are.

- **Nine in the third place:** One worthy of power is active all day, yet still anxious at night. Danger but no blame.

- **Nine in the fourth place:** Back and forth at the edge of an abyss. No blame.
  Indecision when faced with a great and dangerous choice is normal. Do not blame yourself if you must pause before the leap.

- **Nine in the fifth place:** The dragon flies in the sky. Seek the advice of someone greater than yourself.

- **Nine at the top:** An arrogant dragon will have regrets. *Even the best person can overdo it. Stay humble and seek and heed others' advice. You will regret it if you don't.*

- **All nines:** You meet a group of dragons without a head. Good fortune.

Image

Sky upon sky: the image of the creative. You should be like this, continually strengthening yourself.

The motions within the sky are inexorable and untiring. By understanding the kinds of regular changes in the sky, both the apparently immutable sun, moon, and stars and the constantly changing weather, we may come to have a better understanding of the kinds of changes which occur among human beings. Some phenomena seem endless and unchanging, but in fact even the daily reappearance of the sun varies from day to day as the seasons follow one another. We may not be particularly aware of such slow changes, but eventually we feel their impact. In a similar but opposite way, the vagaries of wind and rain may sometimes seem utterly unpredictable, but in fact these too occur within relatively predictable parameters. Few decades go by without at least one year of drought. In low-lying terrain, floods are always possible. Just as we need an emergency fund for the inevitable emergencies of home, health, and car, we need to be prepared for a full range of changes within our lives. As we observe and live through them, we discover more and less fruitful times for action, persistence, or retreat.

This first hexagram has been associated with extremely auspicious times and people, with creativity and leadership. Yet not all of the lines counsel action, and several remind us that the greatest leaders have heeded the advice of others.

Shaughnessy, 38, 39, 287–288.
Lynn, 129–142.
Wilhelm/Baynes, 3–10.

(kūn) Earth, The Receptive

The receptive. Success which flows. A mare's persistence is effective.* One worthy of power has a destination. First, you go astray, and then you attain it. You will benefit by having friends in the southwest, and by losing friends in the northeast. [If you are] peaceful and steadfast, good fortune.

- Six in the first place: You tread on frost and know that hard ice is near.

- Six in the second place: Whether going straight ahead or turning to the side, great. [Even] without practice nothing is ineffective.

- Six in the third place: If you efface your best qualities, you can persevere. When you serve the king's business, what does not succeed ends.
  Though your own projects may not succeed, you may bring important affairs to a successful end.

- **Six in the fourth place**: The sack is tied shut. No blame; no glory.

- **Six in the fifth place**: Yellow skirt or trousers. Continuing good fortune.

- **Six at the top**: If dragons fight in the open fields [between city and countryside], their blood will be dark yellow.

- **All sixes**: It is always effective to persevere.

Image

Earth's strength: the image of receptivity. Thus you should deepen your moral strengths and bear your burdens.

The earth holds and nurtures life with supreme constancy. It is always beneath us, always supporting us. Despite the vagaries of life, this mother of us all is constant. If the earth shifts, it breaks the roots bringing nourishment to the plants within it. Then growth is disrupted, crops die, and people starve. Fortunately, such occasions are very rare. This is a time to contemplate the solidity and stability of the earth, and the ways in which such firmness nurtures life. In human terms, this means remaining firm in our commitment to the completion of the current task. It is by bearing responsibilities that we discover our hidden strengths and ways of overcoming weaknesses. A mother learns new skills and discovers new strengths within her as she continues her care for her child throughout the years. Similarly, we need to learn to practice constancy and receptivity in order to nurture the growth of our souls and our moral strengths.

* Or, *the mare divines effectively.* The word translated here as "persistence" also means "to consult by divining." Since it is hard to imagine a horse engaged in prognostication, "persistence" seems the more likely meaning here and elsewhere. Within the context of *Yijing* usage, the meanings are actually not that far apart, since divining was often used to verify decisions that were nearly complete.

Shaughnessy, 102–103, 304–305.
Lynn, 142–151.
Wilhelm/Baynes, 10–15.

(zhūn) Sprouting

Sprouting ensures continuing growth. Persistence is effective; don't start a journey now. It is good to delegate responsibilities to those you trust.

- Nine in the first place: Pacing back and forth. Persisting where you are is effective, as is appointing helpers.

- Six in the second place: Sprouting like going in circles. Riding a horse but going in circles. When a bandit seeks to marry a woman, she must persist in saying no. But after ten years, then the word marriage.

- Six in the third place: If you hunt deer without a guide, you find yourself lost in the midst of a forest. It is better to give up rather than try to win in this situation. If you move forward, trouble.

- Six in the fourth place: Riding a horse, going in circles. Seek marriage. Moving forward brings good fortune. Nothing is ineffective.

- **Nine in the fifth place:** Sprouting eases your way. If you persist with small things, good fortune. If you persist with the great, misfortune.

- **Six at the top:** Riding the horse in circles. You shed ceaseless, bloody tears.

Image

Clouds and thunder: the image of sprouting. You should set strong warp strings to the loom.

Clouds and thunder were welcome signs on the north China plains, where rainfall was scarce and too much sun could spell death for crops and people. Although the clouds darken the light for a time, and the thunder may be frightening, they usually signal the arrival of the rain necessary for growing things. Similarly, stringing a loom with the long warp threads which will provide strength to a fabric is a difficult process, requiring more than one person to accomplish it. This is a time of new growth and of setting the stage for further growth. This stage usually includes difficulties, but surmounting them will result in a framework, an environment, which will support sustained growth and productivity.

The character that names this hexagram depicts a sprout, a seedling at the stage when, after developing its roots, it has just managed to pierce the crust of the earth and push its first tendril above ground. Many of us can remember a childhood experience of watching a bean go through this process in a clear container, so that we could see the roots developing within the earth. What is visible above ground looks fairly pathetic. The sprout is pallid and weak, bent over and exhausted from the effort of pushing through the earth. We have all had times when we have felt just as exhausted by persistent efforts which have seemed to accomplish little. But the gardener knows that this plant will live, since it has finally attained access to all the sources of energy it needs, from sun and sky as well as from the earth.

A secondary aspect of this stage is delegation. The Zhou kings, who consulted the forerunner of the *Book of Changes*, reigned for nearly eight hundred years but they never tried to rule their entire kingdom directly. They kept a small amount of land under their direct control, enough for their immediate needs, and delegated the supervision of the vast majority of their domains to their relatives, making them subordinate lords, which they enfiefed as dukes. A modern parallel would be the delegation of responsibilities for a project to those worthy of your long-term trust and a fair amount of autonomy.

The lines of the hexagram make it clear that we are not expected to go it alone. Even the greatest person, with the most developed wisdom and self-control, cannot succeed without guides, just as a ruler going hunting requires expert assistance for a successful hunt. If trustworthy help is not available, it is usually better to postpone attempts to move ahead. However, if someone is so committed to us that they have stood by us for ten years, without a commitment on our side, then they are not thieves but truly sincere about spending their lives with us. We need this kind of ally, but we also need to avoid people who might rob us.

Shaughnessy, 82–83, 298–299.
Lynn, 152–158.
Wilhelm/Baynes, 16–20.

4 蒙 (méng) New Grass

Success. It is not I who seek the youth green as grass. The young one seeks me. At first, I explain it. A third [request] is a blasphemy. If you blaspheme, I do not tell. Yet persistence pays.

- **Six in the first place:** The unfolding of the new grass. Applying punishments can benefit another. With restraints removed, you move ahead with difficulty.

- **Nine in the second place:** Surrounding. The young grass: good fortune. Finding a mate for your child: good fortune, as your child sets up a family home.

- **Six in the third place:** Do not grab a woman, but seek out someone able to husband wealth. If you do not possess your self, nothing you do is effective.

- **Six in the fourth place:** Trapped by the young grass [your ignorance or immaturity]: trouble.

- **Six in the fifth place:** A child is immature as young grass. Good fortune.

- **Nine at the top:** Training the young through punishments. Becoming a robber does not pay; defending against robbers does pay.

Image

At the foot of the mountain, a spring gushes forth: the image of being as young as new grass. You should grow through accepting instruction about moral strengths.

New grass rises from the earth as inexorably as a spring continues to pulse water up at the base of a mountain. Though it brings life-giving water, the mountain dwarfs the spring, just as the tender shoots of new grass are mere fuzz on the plains. The new grass has immense potential for productive life, but at this stage it is still fragile and in need of nurturing, just as a young child needs instruction in order to lay the foundations for a good life. Such instruction may feel as restraining as handcuffs or leg shackles at times, but it is essential.

For example, children need to learn to share and to become aware of the needs and rights of others as well as themselves. Only by being alive to others' needs, fears, and hopes can we find effective ways to satisfy our own needs. Babies are loveable, but cannot recognize that it is not always convenient for their mothers to nurse them. We all need to grow beyond the stage of instinctive reactions to an ability to act with moral strength, restraining our own needs until they harmonize with others.

This hexagram has been translated as "youthful folly," and it does represent the sometime foolish actions of the very young. Some restraint is protective, and at first it must come from outside, but in a gentle manner that nurtures the ability to internalize these restraints so that external fetters are no longer necessary, and mature adults are able to make their own decisions about appropriate actions, words, and times for action and inaction.

Shaughnessy, 62–63, 294.
Lynn, 158–165.
Wilhelm/Baynes, 20–24.

(xū) Waiting

If you have sincerity, your successes will be broad and wide. Persisting brings good fortune. You do well to cross the great river.

- Nine in the first place: Waiting in the country just outside the city. Persistent endurance will benefit you, with no blame.

- Nine in the second place: Waiting on the sand. The small-minded may gossip, but in the end good fortune comes.

- Nine in the third place: Waiting in the mud. Robbers arrive. *You are mired in this problem, tempting others to rob you while you are so vulnerable.*

- Six in the fourth place: Waiting in blood: get out of this pit!

- Nine in the fifth place: Waiting with food and drink: to persist brings good fortune.

- **Six at the top**: You enter into a cave [your modest home] and three uninvited guests arrive. If you treat them with respect, in the end good fortune will come.

Image

Rain atop the sky: the image of waiting. You should find peace and joy in drinking and eating.

Waiting is rarely easy. In this situation, the needed rain is in sight, but the clouds are high in the sky and have not yet descended to the parched earth where they are needed. At such times, there is nothing we can do to hasten their arrival, so we should instead focus on the simple daily pleasures of eating and drinking, and find peace in them while we wait. In this way, we can keep up our strength physically, and restore ourselves psychically by recognizing and savoring the security and joy we find in meeting present needs. This can be a real discipline when we know major problems must be dealt with, and that the means for doing so can be seen. But we will need strength in both body and mind when this period of waiting comes to an end, as it will.

The agricultural image is of a crop in need of rain, which has not yet fallen. Yet the anxious farmer needs the reminder that there is enough food and drink for this day, and that it should be consumed and enjoyed as a part of the process of waiting. To the Chinese, this situation seemed analogous to the time just before the Zhou conquest of the oppressive Shang rulers. The good King Wu already ruled his own tribe and had begun to muster his forces, but was not strong enough yet to attack Shang.

The individual lines describe six different environments for this kind of waiting, some favorable, some not. Although elsewhere in the *Changes* energetic progress is encouraged, here sustenance and perseverance are the preferred responses. Enjoy what you have now, share it gladly with visitors even if it seems meager. A time of change is coming, but not today.

Shaughnessy, 72–73, 296.
Lynn, 165–170.
Wilhelm/Baynes, 24–26.

訟

6

(sòng) Strife

Strife. If you are sincere in your regrets, take the middle way, and you will have good fortune. If you persist to the end, you face disaster. You ought to seek the advice of someone greater than you are. Crossing the great river [attempting a major change] is ineffective.

- Six in the first place: If you do not prolong this dispute, petty people may talk, but in the end you will have good fortune.

- Nine in the second place: You cannot win this dispute. Return home and escape. [Even though your resources may be limited], to a city of [only] three hundred families, there will be no disaster.

- Six in the third place: Feeding on old virtues. If you persist, danger and good fortune. But the king's business will not be achieved. [matters affecting many people will come to nothing]

- **Nine in the fourth place:** Unsuccessful in strife. Turn back, submit to what is mandated. But if you change your aims and then persevere, good fortune.

- **Nine in the fifth place:** Strife at the source. Good fortune.

- **Nine at the top:** The belt of noble rank is bestowed, but in the end it is taken away three times in a single day.
  You may seem the winner at first, but your reward will be taken back again and again.

Image

The sky with water pouring down: the image of strife. You should take on a new direction only after careful consideration of its beginnings.

When water gushes from the sky, it is not a good time to start building anything. In addition to the normal reasons for delaying building, in early China, great structures were built on foundations of tamped earth. Trying to gather soil, fill the form with it, and tamp it down would be impossible during a deluge, since the soil would turn into liquid mud. Trying to build something solid with materials that dissolve is as foolish as trying to achieve something significant in the middle of a dispute. This is a time to take shelter and cut your losses, not move ahead.

Living in a time of frequent warfare and political instability, the early Chinese were all too aware of the dangers of strife, and of the difficulties of avoiding it. For this reason, this hexagram emphasizes the dangers of contentiousness, and the fact that it is rarely productive and often destructive, even to those who seem at first to triumph. It advises that you recognize when you have lost or are likely to lose, and to withdraw from the struggle even if small-minded people ridicule you for doing so. Only one of the six lines predicts a positive outcome, and that relates to difficulties associated with the source or beginnings; that is, with the most basic of issues, dealt with in the only timely manner, at the beginning. Thus, if you are planning a new venture and find basic disagreements on aims or methods with your colleagues, these need to be addressed lest these disagreements render all future efforts flawed. However, in almost every other situation, a time of strife is not auspicious, not a good time to try to move ahead, since almost any venture will fail under these conditions. You may need to wait, to seek some alternative to the one you are considering.

Shaughnessy, 46–47, 290.
Lynn, 170–177.
Wilhelm/Baynes, 28–31.

7 師

(shī) With a Multitude of Followers

The army [or multitude] persists. With a forceful commander, no blame.

- Six in the first place: The army moves out in cadence [in step with one another, to the beating of the drums marshalling them]. They are not slaves: disaster.

- Nine in the second place: In the center of the multitude lies good fortune without blame. The ruler issues directives three times.

- Six in the third place: The army has wagons full of corpses. Disaster.

- Six in the fourth place: The multitude camps on the left without blame.

- Six in the fifth place: When your crop fields are full of game, shooting them is effective and blameless. [However,] if the elder son leads the troops into battle so that the younger son must take charge of carts full of the dead, persevering brings disaster.

- **Six at the top**: A great leader has directives to open up sub-kingdoms and nourish families. But a petty man does not.

Image

The earth holds water within itself: the image of an army of followers. You should cherish and support the people entrusted to you.

This is the opposite of the preceding hexagram, contention, a time when there is so much squabbling and litigation that even apparent victories result in multiple losses. In this situation, there is unity among a multitude numerous enough and united enough in aims and in mutual trust to be able to take major effective actions. It is only with a vast multitude of followers and with full unity among them that effective political action is possible. For this reason, King Wu delayed his conquest of the Shang until he knew that his forces were fully sufficient. Even then, the Shang army was many times larger than his. But cruel and unpredictable Shang tyrants had made loyalty to them so costly by this time that the outnumbered Zhou forces triumphed. Still the memory of being outnumbered must have haunted later Zhou leaders and led to the comments here.

Shaughnessy, 110–111, 305–306.
Lynn, 177–183.
Wilhelm/Baynes, 31–35.

(bǐ) Closeness with Others

Closeness with others. Good fortune. Consult the oracle again. If you are steadfast from the beginning, no blame. When upsets come from every side, the one who arrives late will meet disaster.

- Six in the first place: If there is sincerity, keeping close to them will not bring blame. Having sincerity is like having a pot filled. Even if harm comes in the end, you will find good fortune.

- Six in the second place: A trusted ally from within. Persistence brings good fortune.

- Six in the third place: Close to the wrong person.

- Six in the fourth place: Close to someone from the outside. Persistence brings good fortune.

- Nine in the fifth place: Openly shown closeness. When rulers hunt, they drive the prey three times [into a narrow escape route] but let the first wave of animals escape. Do not frighten the people of your own town. Good fortune.

- **Six at the top:** When your allies lack a leader, misfortune.

Image

Above the earth, water: the image of being close to allies. The first rulers established subsidiary realms and treated others as members of their own families.

When water lies on the earth, the two are so closely bound that they seep into one another. Because both meet so closely, plants can grow. This is how close true allies should be. The Zhou kings did not try to govern alone. Instead, they delegated the control of most of their realm to feudal lords, many of whom were relatives. Each of these had full autonomy within his fief and passed this leadership on to his descendants. This hexagram celebrates enduring and open alliances and the careful selection and later steadfastness that make them productive. It returns to a common theme in the book: the need to delegate effectively and in a timely manner; that is, when great projects are begun. Then those allies should be retained with the same trust and forbearance given to those allies we are given by the accidents of birth, our families.

Wise leaders avoid greed. They delegate to the leaders of groups beneath them, giving them quite a lot of autonomy, treating them as well as they would their own families, rewarding those who deserve continuing trust, and being extremely selective in reaping profits, down-sizing, and punishing errors. This apparently loose control is in fact more practical than constant surveillance and taking profits as quickly as possible. It fosters a flow in the organization, enough control and harvesting to meet real needs. By avoiding rapid changes, sustainable prosperity and ongoing relationships are possible.

Shaughnessy, 74–75, 297.
Lynn, 184–190.
Wilhelm/Baynes, 35–39.

9 小畜 (xiǎo chù) The Smaller Herd

The smaller herd. Success. Dense clouds but no rain from our western pastures.

- **Nine in the first place:** Returning from the way. How could there be blame? Good fortune.

- **Nine in the second place:** Led back. Good fortune.

- **Nine in the third place:** Cart and axle-strut part. Husband and wife have opposing views.

- **Six in the fourth place:** There is sincerity. Blood goes away; anxiety departs. No blame.

- **Nine in the fifth place:** There is linked sincerity. Prosper together with your neighbors.

- **Nine at the top:** Already there is rain, already in its place. Esteemed for moral strength and honored by a carriage. For a woman, persistence brings danger. The day after the full moon, one worthy of power starts a campaign: misfortune.

Image

**The wind moves above the sky: the image of a small herd.
You should cultivate the moral strengths in civility.**

The free movement of the winds in the highest levels of the sky is likened to the mobility of a small herd of domesticated animals, and this to the necessary mustering and cultivation of virtues. This hexagram, like another, refers to the period preceding the Zhou conquest of Shang; that is, to a time of the greatest promise, not yet fulfilled. It is nearly the turning point, but the forces of evil remain powerful and in control. There is great hope, but as yet no certainty about the outcome of the forthcoming struggle. This is, therefore, a time for caution, for making sure that all is well within one's closest relationships and most essential tools. For even the best person, the situation, though increasingly positive, is still too dangerous for decisive action to be taken, or for determined persistence to be perceptible.

While major decisions and decisive action are inappropriate at this time, there is still work to be done, and great hope for the future. Current tasks may seem mundane. But tasks like maintaining your vehicle, and making sure you and those closest to you really see eye to eye are absolutely essential. Once action begins, your safety will depend on the reliability of your transport and your alliances. Since you cannot afford to stop to repair them once rapid progress starts, do so now, even if no major trouble is yet evident. Thus you lay the foundations for unimpeded and less dangerous progress in the more propitious time ahead.

Shaughnessy, 152–153, 318–319.
Lynn, 191–199.
Wilhelm/Baynes, 40–43.

履 ䷉

10

(lǚ) Stepping

Stepping on the tail of a tiger. It does not bite you. Success.

- **Nine in the first place:** Simple walking. In going, no blame.

- **Nine in the second place:** Walking the road with sincerity. The person in darkness persists; good fortune.

- **Six in the third place:** The half-blind can see; the half-lame can walk. When you step on the tail of a tiger, it bites the person. Misfortune: the warrior acts like a great lord.

- **Nine in the fourth place:** Stepping on the tail of a tiger, fearfully, fearfully. But in the end, good fortune.

- **Nine in the fifth place:** Resolute walking: persistence, danger.

- **Nine at the top:** Looking at the step, examining the luck, she completes the circle. Great good fortune.

Image

The sky above, a lake below: the image of taking a step. You should differentiate carefully between high and low, and define the people's goals.

While the image speaks of a lake lying below the sky, and of the importance of differentiating between things and people which are high or low, the dominant image of the original hexagram is more vivid: stepping on the tail of a tiger. Such a terrifying misstep could easily cause death. You may have antagonized a powerful person and made a dangerous enemy. Even if you feel terrified, avoid panic. Take time to see the situation clearly in all its levels, and to remember the needs of all those you serve before taking further actions.

This hexagram reminds us that even terrifying beasts like offended tigers are not always destructive. Here, the tiger bites in only one of the six possible phases (lines). And even in that line we are reminded that the half-blind can see and that the lame can walk. Most frightening situations are not total catastrophes.

There are times when you may arouse immense hostility and yet escape unscathed. Remaining alert is essential, as is an avoidance of panic. We may be able to cope with this situation and walk away unharmed, just as people sometimes walk away from sudden encounters with other ferocious beasts. Now that you have aroused the tiger, watch him carefully, whether he be beast, human, or an urge within you. Tread softly but do not run away. Try to see yourself and the other clearly and proceed cautiously.

Once the situation has passed (nine at the top), review the steps that brought you into and out of this position, and the results on multiple levels. By remaining as aloof as the sky above is from a deep lake below, you may cultivate the stillness which makes seeing clearly possible in either air or water.

Shaughnessy, 44, 45, 289–290.
Lynn, 200–205.
Wilhelm/Baynes, 44–47.

11 泰 ䷊

(tài) Peace

The petty depart; the great arrive. Good fortune; success.

- Nine in the first place: When you uproot rushes, they come up in a bundle. Move forward: success.

- Nine in the second place: Embrace the flow, ford the stream. Do not forget what is far away. Although friends may be lost, you attain rewards by taking the middle way.

- Nine in the third place: Nothing level without some rising; no leaving without a return. If in difficulties you persist, no regrets. Without anxiety, sincerity [returning]. In eating, good fortune.

- Six in the fourth place: Fluttering wings. Do not enrich yourself by using your neighbors. Don't admonish [them but] use sincerity. [Or If you do not admonish the neighbors, they are more likely be sincere.]

- **Six in the fifth place:** The Lord Yi helped his younger sister marry and attain blessings. Good fortune flows.

- **Six at the top:** When the walls of your city collapse into the moat [eliminating all your defenses], don't muster your troops. Issue commands only in your own city. Persistence brings trouble.

Image

Sky and earth interact: peace. Thus the queen guides the natural forces of both sky and earth, assisting them into harmony by [gathering] the people to her right and left.

As earth and sky interact with one another, all things are created. This kind of peace is the reverse of immobility. Instead it is a time when those above are receptive to those beneath them, so that creativity rises up in abundance. When mother, teacher, manager, or leader hears and heeds her children, students, or co-workers, she acts as a life-giving refuge which provides protection to new lives when they are as vulnerable as fledglings or new kings. Only the greatest leaders are capable of the self-restraint and generosity required for true receptivity to those beneath them. But such leaders gain a realistic, nuanced picture of the realities they face and elicit sincere and creative loyalty. Authoritarian rulers, listening only to sycophants, quash creativity and real loyalty, bringing destruction to their people. Because Mao refused to listen to those who brought unwelcome news of bad harvests during the Great Leap Forward, millions perished.

Peace here is not static, not everyone stuck in their "proper places," but out of their usual places and therefore moving towards one another. Here earth, the receptive, lies above the creative, usually associated with the sky above. It is because leaders are willing to be humble and their subordinates dare to create that a fecund peace can be attained.

Xunzi wrote that people must guide natural forces into creative relationships. First, an educated person recognizes her limits, what she can and cannot control, and applies her analysis to the great forces in a positive way. Thus people have learned not to ask for winter not to come but to raise, preserve, and store food in preparation for scarce times. Great rulers expected and prepared for floodwaters and long droughts, building cities on high ground, leaving water meadows for overflows and building dikes to guide the floodwaters. They built storehouses and filled them with grain in years of plenty in order to prepare for the inevitable, eventual arrival of years of scarcity. Confident that they would be fed, the people could be more productive and avoid the need for theft.

Shaughnessy, 104–105, 304–305.
Lynn, 205–211.
Wilhelm/Baynes, 48–52.

12 否 (pǐ) Obstruction (Stagnation)

Others, who are evil, are obstructing you. You should not persist: it will not work out. The great depart; the petty gain. This is a time of great losses and small gains. Do not persist in this direction.

- Six in the first place: When you pull up the rushes, they come up clumped together. If you persist, you will find good fortune and success.

- Six in the second place: While accepting orders, inferior people prosper; great people do not. Success.

- Six in the third place: Accept the sadness.

- Nine in the fourth place: Under orders, blameless. The many depend on each other, then prosper.

- Nine in the fifth place: The stagnation ends. For a great one, good fortune. Lost? Lost? Tie it to a clump of mulberry shoots.

- **Nine at the top:** The stagnation collapses. First blockage, later joy.

Image

Earth and sky are out of alignment: the image of stagnation. You should restrain your own strength to escape difficulties. You cannot accept honors or a salary under these conditions.

Here such stasis goes against the natural process of unceasing change. Obstructing the flow of change is stultifying. Even if we feel comfortable, as we have been, we need to move out of accustomed places and towards one another if we are to be creative. If we are to grow, like plants we need to move toward our suns with the support of those growing around us.

Sky rests above earth, and fails to interact with it. When the strong rule the weak, separation leads to stagnation. While such a situation may seem stable, it is dangerous. Growth comes when weak and strong interact, and change continues.

When many obstacles bar your progress, this may be due to external conditions rather than your own strengths or weaknesses. When the time is out of joint, or malevolent people are in power, even natural forces cannot interact creatively. You must accept orders; you may not be able to refuse them. In such conditions, there is no shame in doing so until good actions have a greater probability of success. You may need to watch nasty people prosper and avoid involvement (as well as promotion and the admiration of others.) Remember that no condition, however harsh, lasts forever. Preserve yourself and your integrity as well as you can, lying low and living simply until the obstruction or stagnation ceases, as it will eventually. This hexagram is unclear as to whether you should act to hasten the end of wrongdoings or simply wait until they dissolve of themselves. Different lines provide different advice, suggesting that even in times of stagnation, some moments are more propitious than others.

Shaughnessy, 40–41, 288.
Lynn, 211–215.
Wilhelm/Baynes, 52–55.

(tóng rén) Friendship

Meeting with others in open fields. Success. It is effective to cross the great river. Persistence is effective for one worthy of power.

- **Nine in the first place:** Fellowship with others at the gate. No blame.

- **Six in the second place:** Fellowship with others in the clan. Difficulties.

- **Nine in the third place:** Encamp the army in the woods. They will climb the high hill. For three years, do not send them out [to fight].

- **Nine in the fourth place:** Occupy the city wall but do not conquer them. Good fortune.

- **Nine in the fifth place:** Fellowship with others: first sobbing, later laughter. The great multitude conquers because it works together.

- **Nine at the top:** Fellowship with others on the outskirts of town. No remorse.

Image

The sky blazes with fire: the image of fellowship with others. You should observe differences in all things, even in friendship.

Fire below the sky, the sun's spreading illumination, represents the kind of openness required of long-lasting friendships and alliances. This clarity also reveals differences that must be recognized, appreciated, and used appropriately. With such a balance, this can be a good time to make a major change.

Shaughnessy, 48–49, 290–291.
Lynn, 216–222.
Wilhelm/Baynes, 56–59.

14 大有 ䷍

(dà yǒu) Great Possession

Great possession. Supreme success.

- **Nine in the first place:** No encounters with harm. No blame. There may be difficulties, but no blame.

- **Nine in the second place:** Great wagons, used to transport goods. You have a destination. No blame.

- **Nine in the third place:** A duke pays tribute to the ruler. Lesser people cannot do this.

- **Nine in the fourth place:** If you reject boastfulness, no blame.

- **Six in the fifth place:** Sincere mutual respect. Dangerous, fortunate.

- **Nine at the top:** From the sky above, a blessing on you. Good fortune. Nothing will be ineffectual.

Image

Fire above the sky: the image of great possessions. You should retard evil and promote goodness, following Nature's essential will.

When fire is above the sky, it is visible near and far, illuminating all below it. This is a time of brilliance, but not necessarily a time for relaxation or overconfidence. With great possessions come great responsibilities to one's neighbors, and to the highest powers. Remember that this too shall pass, and act in a way that you will not regret when people below you now may be above you later. If you avoid boasting and share, you will minimize the envy your good fortune will arouse.

You may want to read hexagrams 28 and 55, which also describe times of abundance, the following hexagram 15 on modesty, and remember the top line of hexagram 1: even someone as great as a dragon will have reasons for regret if he is arrogant. A time of abundance is also a good time to limit your consumption, and save generously for leaner times, which will inevitably come, since no triumph lasts forever.

Shaughnessy, 136–137, 313.
Lynn, 223–229.
Wilhelm/Baynes, 59–63.

(qiān) Modesty

Success. For one worthy of power, an end.

- **Six in the first place:** Modest again and again: one worthy of power. You may cross the great river [make a major change]. Good fortune.

- **Six in the second place:** The bird sings of modesty. Persistence brings good fortune.

- **Nine in the third place:** At work, modesty: one worthy of power. At the end, good fortune.

- **Six in the fourth place:** Nothing that is not effective. Practice in modesty.

- **Six in the fifth place:** Not rich by using her neighbors. A decisive move can be used effectively. Nothing is ineffectual.

- **Six at the top:** The bird sings of modesty. It is effective to use the actions of multitudes to advance on city and state.

Image

In the midst of the earth, a mountain: modesty. You should reduce the numbers of things that are too numerous and increase things in short supply, to bring balance.

Even the highest mountain rises out of the earth, which holds it in place. Even the most elevated personage depends on many others for sustenance and health. Modesty is the crucial quality that enables us to remember our own limits and to value all we can learn from others. History is full of rulers who forgot this and lost everything. Those with little must be given more. Those with an excess need less.

Shaughnessy, 106–107, 305.
Lynn, 229–234.
Wilhelm/Baynes, 63–67.

16 餘 ䷏

(yú) Excess

It is effective to appoint trusted helpers (literally, to establish subordinate leaders in their domains), and to set the troops marching.

- Six in the first place: Crying out excessively: misfortune.

- Six in the second place: Scratched on a rock, but not lasting until day's end. Persistence brings good fortune.

- Six in the third place: If over-confident, regret. If hesitant, regret.

- Nine in the fourth place: Real contentment. Great attainments. No doubts. Friends gather as a hairpin [gathers long hair.] (R)*
Real excess. Great with attainments. Don't doubt: Friends armored with slander. (M)*

- Six in the fifth place: Persevere when ill. It may last long, but not be fatal.

- **Six at the top:** At sunset, excess achieved. There is information but no blame.

Image

Thunder rolls, the earth shakes: the image of excess (or enjoyment). Thus former rulers made music, ennobled the virtuous, and made splendid offerings to the Lord on High, in order to be deemed worthy of their ancestors.

Early Chinese envisaged earthquakes as thunder breaking out of the earth. Having excess is likened to such an upheaval. Perhaps this is because they were so used to times of scarcity. When we are overwhelmed by excess or by joy, we may be tempted to simply bask in this pleasant anomaly. This image reminds us that having much can be dangerous if it is not shared in appropriate ways. With increased wealth or power come responsibilities too great for one person to control alone. We need to find trustworthy allies and delegate powers to them, just as the new Zhou kings enfiefed their relatives with allied but autonomous realms. New musical forms should be used to express our joy in ways that can endure and knit together the community into a multi-dimensional harmony. Some of the excess must also be used to recognize good people and to sacrifice to the Higher Power. If, in a time of excess, we replace broken systems with new forms of organization, song, and rites of praise for both people and whatever is above us, we may move ahead with our plans effectively.

It is hard to remember that having too much can be as upsetting to our lives as an earthquake is to the land broken by it. New forms must be created to delegate excessive responsibilities to subordinates worthy of long-term trust, to recognize the good in others, and to express in music the joy that comes from abundance.

Some of the excess must be sacrificed to the Highest Power, then shared among those entrusted with the care of the many. Only in this way can we be worthy of all those before us who have prepared the way for the changes brought by excess.

* R: in received text; M: in Mawangdui text.

Shaughnessy, 90–91, 301.
Lynn, 235–241.
Wilhelm/Baynes, 67–71.

17 隨䷐

(suí) Following

From the beginning, success. It is effective to persist; no blame.

- Nine in the first place: The office is notified. Persisting brings good fortune. Going out of the gate [of one's home] to socialize, there is achievement.

- Six in the second place: If you tie up the boy, you lose the man.

- Six in the third place: If you tie up the man, you lose the boy. Following has seeking and getting; it is effective to persist where you dwell.

- Nine in the fourth place: Following has a catch (or servant); Persistence brings misfortune. When there is a return to the way, in order to swear an oath, how could there be blame?

- Nine in the fifth place: Return to joy/excellence: good fortune.

- **Six at the top:** If you tie them up, then set them free. The ruler uses a sacrifice done at the western mountain.

Image
Within the lake, thunder: the image of following. Thus you should go inside and rest quietly in the evening.

Here thunder is within the lake, rather than coming forth out of the earth, and the image is of following rather than of leading. After the thunder passes, the lake reverts to its accustomed calm, whereas after an earthquake the land does not return to its original location. A convulsion of a liquid element is not long lasting, just as the troubles of an active day usually die down toward the end of the day, or the intense activity of heavy responsibilities fades away into the more relaxed and restful life of a person who no longer has much importance in deciding the events of the day.

Shaughnessy, 130–131, 311–312.
Lynn, 241–248.
Wilhelm/Baynes, 71–75.

18 箇 ䷅ (gǔ) Branching Out

Good fortune and success. Fording the great river is effective. Before the start of a ten-day period,* three days. After the first of ten days, three days.

- Six in the first place: Stemming from father's branch: having a child who is crafty. No blame, but trouble. In the end, good fortune.

- Nine in the second place: Stem of mother's branch: you cannot persist.

- Nine in the third place: Stem of father's branch: few have regrets. No great blame.

- Six in the fourth place: Water over father's branch: going to see. Trouble.

- Six in the fifth place: Stem of father's branch: using a cart.

- **Nine at the top:** Glorifying your own deeds instead of bringing admiration to ruler and lords. Misfortune.

Image

Below the mountain, a wind: the image of branching out. You should stir up the people and nourish moral strengths.

When a bamboo grows, its stems send off branches. This is likened to the winds that blow around the foot of a mountain. This is a healthy part of natural growth and change. The focus of the lines seems to be on the stems, paternal or maternal, and on the types of growth the branches (or children) may provide for the whole plant (family).

For many centuries, another character with the same sound was accepted as the title of this hexagram. Its emphasis was also on changes from one's parents' pasts, but this positive aspect was overshadowed by the vividness of the alternative image: a bowl holding a writhing mass of insects consuming rotten food. However, the older Mawangdui text found in the tomb of a Han duchess makes more sense; that is, it is more consistent within itself in referring to both stems and branches rather than to saving insect-infested food, clearly an impossible (and disgusting) task.

Think instead of a clump of bamboo and the branches from its stems. (The word for *branch* here has the bamboo radical, not the tree radical). What is common to this growing plant and to the winds at the feet of mountains? Both winds and branches seem weaker, yet both are more flexible, than their larger partner. Some branches may need trimming, just as some winds may necessitate windbreaks. Yet life could not continue without some branching, if only to put forth more leaves, just as a climate cannot be salubrious without some wind. We are urged here to encourage others in the development of their capabilities, to feed their desire for what is sound, what has virtue in themselves and in what they can do. Likewise, we are warned that self-promotion at the expense of the whole picture seen by good leaders would be a mistake.

* Ten days was the usual duration of the traditional Chinese "week."

Shaughnessy, 68–69, 295.
Lynn, 248–253.
Wilhelm/Baynes, 75–78.

(lín) The Forest

From the beginning, good fortune. Persistence is effective. When you arrive at the eighth month, there will be misfortune.

- Nine in the first place: The prohibited forest: persistence brings good fortune.

- Nine in the second place: The prohibited forest. Good fortune, nothing that is ineffectual.

- Six in the third place: The sweet forest: not having a destination is effective. Already worried over it, but no blame.

- Six in the fourth place: Nearing the forest: no blame.

- Six in the fifth place: Knowing the forest: what is suitable for a great ruler. Good fortune.

- Six at the top: Thick forest, good fortune without blame.

Image

Over the lake there is earth: the forest. You should be inexhaustible in the sincerity of your thoughts and limitless in offering protection to the people.

The image here is either that of a forest (Mawangdui) or of looking downward, usually construed as overseeing or governing—perhaps related to seeing the forest instead of the trees. Certainly a forest grows well when it is planted in earth fed by subterranean sources of water. Then few droughts are severe enough to kill the trees, and their lives seem inexhaustible, fed by vast aquifers below them. Similarly looking down from the height of a tree should provide perspective and a wider, more comprehensive view of those for whom one is responsible. From this vantage point, one should be able to see workable combinations of people and tasks, and to act with both knowledge and sensitivity to feelings.

Think of the great strength a forest possesses, especially one fed by subterranean springs or streams. In addition to this sustenance, the trees can lean against one another so that strong gusts of wind are far less likely to topple them than a single tree standing alone. Forests were often on land shared by many, and the people were free to gather downed branches and other dead wood to use for their cooking fires. By the fourth century BCE, Mencius had already recognized the dangers of deforestation and erosion. This suggests that such destruction had already occurred in some places by his era; he mentioned a specific hill near a large city.

Shaughnessy, 108–109, 305.
Lynn, 254–259.
Wilhelm/Baynes, 78–81.

20 觀見 ䷓

(guān) Gazing (Contemplation)

The hands have been washed, but they have not yet offered up the sacrifice. There is sincerity and solemnity.

- Six in the first place: The gaze of youth: for a minor person, no blame. For one worthy of authority, difficulties.

- Six in the second place: A peeping gaze: a woman's persistence is effective.

- Six in the third place: Gazing at my life: advances, retreats.

- Six in the fourth place: Gazing at the splendor of the nation: appropriate for the guest of the ruler.

- Nine in the fifth place: Gazing at my life: for one worthy of authority, no blame.

- Nine at the top: Gazing at their lives: for one worthy of authority, no blame.

Image

Winds move over the earth: the image of gazing. Thus former rulers traveled their realms, viewed the people, and issued instructions.

In the same untrammeled way that the winds move over the entire surface of the earth, unhindered by obstacles, undaunted by distance, anyone in a position of responsibility must let her gaze travel far, beyond her own concerns or those of the people who seem to speak most clearly. For this reason, the great and good rulers of China's halcyon past traveled among their people, observing their lives and conditions at close range. In this way, they were able to see for themselves the actual conditions of the people, and to meet many of them. In addition, the people were able to observe the ruler's concern with their lives, and to express their complaints and fears directly. Openness to forthright criticism from even the most lowly was considered essential. Only after learning from observing and listening to the people did these wise rulers dare to formulate their instructions to them.

This hexagram describes a time for gaining a broader perspective, a wider view. Such an endeavor is not always possible, so the time appropriate for it should be seized and used, and the knowledge gained from a wider gaze should be internalized, stored up for times when informed decisions must be made. The various lines of the hexagram describe the gazes of different kinds of people: the young, the petty, the responsible. Such contemplative gazing is essential for the continuing growth of our best qualities. At times we need to concentrate our gaze on the advances and retreats of our own lives, on the needs of our country, or on others' lives. Each changing line suggests a different direction, but all encourage a broader vision, and clear, thoughtful viewing of many people and factors before advising others or making major decisions, or acting upon them.

Shaughnessy, 154–155, 319.
Lynn, 260–265.
Wilhelm/Baynes, 82–85.

21 噬嗑 ䷔

(shì kè) Taking a Bite

Biting until your teeth touch. Success. It is effective to apply punishments.

- **Nine in the first place:** Crooked fetters, a severed foot. [Yet] no blame.

- **Six in the second place:** Biting into tender meat; a severed nose. No blame.

- **Six in the third place:** Biting into dried meat; encountering poison. A few dangers but no blame.

- **Nine in the fourth place:** Biting into dried meat, getting a metal arrowhead. Persisting during difficulties is effective. Good fortune.

- **Six in the fifth place:** Biting into dried meat, getting poison. Persistence brings danger but no blame.

- **Nine at the top:** Wearing the wooden yoke of a criminal; losing an ear. Misfortune.

Image

Thunder and lightning, the image of biting until the teeth touch. In this way the rulers of the past clarified punishments and adjust the laws.

Thunder and lightning startle us and get the attention of many people in a large area. Biting off a piece of meat is also a visible, decisive act much briefer than the rest of the digestive process, especially in a society where meat was rarely eaten. For these reasons, both are used here as images of the punishments which must occasionally be inflicted by the state in order to deter others from the destructive behaviors that bring destruction to the body of anyone who commits them.

In early China, meat was primarily consumed at the feasts of the elite after the hunting, which was the prerogative of the ruler and his honored guests, and after the sacrifice of animals in religious rituals, where the meat was then shared by the ruler with his highest vassals as an emblem of his entrusting portions of his food-producing lands to them. Preserved meat was highly prized; Confucius accepted it as tuition. Being able to bite into meat can also be seen as a measure of one's good health, strength, and, implicitly, competence.

Similarly, criminal punishments in early China were brief, shocking, and widely visible. Instead of imprisoning criminals for long periods with the hope that they would become penitent, the Chinese usually disfigured and released them. Some of these punishments are mentioned here: cutting off a nose, foot, or ear, or being forced to wear wrist or ankle irons or a heavy wooden yoke around the neck, burdening the shoulders and making lying down difficult or impossible.

These images are hardly reassuring or encouraging, but they probably refer to occasions when an official was forced to mete out punishments, not to having them inflicted on oneself, since this was rarely done to members of the elite. So, although only one line of the hexagram is actually favorable, only one is completely unfavorable. Maintaining the analogy with the act of taking a bite of meat, the situation described here is one in which you are forced to deal decisively with others' acts of cruelty to others.

Shaughnessy, 146–147, 317–318.
Lynn, 266–272.
Wilhelm/Baynes, 86–89.

22 賁 ䷕

(bì) Elegance

Success. In small matters, it is appropriate to go.

- Nine in the first place: Elegant your feet. Discarding the chariot and walking.

- Six in the second place: Elegant your cheek.

- Nine in the third place: Such elegance, such luster! Endless constancy, good fortune.

- Six in the fourth place: Such elegance, such fairness! So like a white horse, be constant.

- Six in the fifth place: The elegance of a hillside garden. To the east, the bolt of silk is in tatters. Trouble, but in the end, good fortune.

- Nine at the top: Simple elegance, without blame.

Image

Below the mountain, there is a fire: the image of elegance. You should clearly understand the varieties of governance, and not dare to judge criminals.

Fire at the foot of a mountain is the image of elegance and grace. Here, the flames remain at its foot, illuminating their immediate area but refraining from consuming wide swaths of timber. Smallness and restraint are praised, and it is suitable to make progress in small matters. But elegance, though pleasant, is insufficient for the accomplishment of great enterprises. Therefore if you are considering making a major change, perhaps you should make some small moves in that direction, but refrain from any life-changing commitment for a while.

Shaughnessy, 64–65, 294.
Lynn, 273–279.
Wilhelm/Baynes, 90–93.

23 剥䷖

(bō) Peeling

It is inappropriate to start a major project [lit., to have someplace to go].

- **Six in the first place:** Peeling the bed to the legs. Obstructed perseverance: misfortune.

- **Six in the second place:** Peeling the good away with disputes. Destroyed persistence: misfortune.

- **Six in the third place:** Peeling it. No blame.

- **Six in the fourth place:** Peeling the bed to the skin; misfortune.

- **Six in the fifth place:** A string of fish. Eating from the courtier's steamer. Nothing fails.

- **Nine at the top:** The fruit with a pit is not eaten. The noble obtain transport; the inferior peels a gourd.

Image

A mountain attached to the earth: the image of peeling.
[When] those above treat those beneath with generosity, they make their own dwellings secure.

When good people are peeled away from a person or a project by disputes, obstructions, or lack of sharing, no project can succeed. A mountain needs to be attached to the earth; peeled from it, it must fall. Likewise, even the greatest person cannot stand alone for long. To flourish, we all need supporters and friends. For this reason, it is necessary to avoid unnecessary conflicts and disputes, and to share the best that is available. Peeled away from others, you can accomplish little.

Shaughnessy, 58–59, 293.
Lynn, 280–285
Wilhelm/Baynes, 93–96.

24 復䷗

(fù) Returning

Success. Going out and coming in without sickness. Burial comes without blame. If you return to the right road: in seven days you come and return. It is good to have a place to go.

- Nine in the first place: Before going too far, return without much regret. Great good fortune.

- Six in the second place: A restful return. Good fortune.

- Six in the third place: A sequence of returns. Danger but no blame.

- Six in the fourth place: Walking in the middle of the road. Returning alone.

- Six in the fifth place: Returning at another's urging, with no regrets.

- **Six at the top:** A lost return. Misfortune. There is a disaster. Putting an army to marching ends in a great defeat involving the leader of the state. Misfortune. For ten years they cannot attack.

Image

Thunder within the earth: the image of returning. Early rulers closed the passes at the winter solstice. Merchants and wanderers did not travel. The queen did not inspect her domain.

An earthquake (thunder within the earth) is used here as an image of returning, a term originally derived from a pictogram of a cooking vessel. Earthquakes displace the stability of the earth, damaging or destroying our homes, threatening all we have. They shake our comfortable assumptions and force us to confront our most basic needs without our customary shelters. Here earthquakes are associated with the perils of traveling at the time of the winter solstice, when China's earliest rulers closed the mountain passes so that merchants and other travelers were forced to stay at home. The queen also refrained from inspecting her domains at such times.

When our lives are shaken to their foundation, we must return to what gives us sustenance. A time of turning is not the right time for aggressive actions, which would only lead to crushing defeats. To others, we may seem to have stopped making progress, and this may be true in a visible, material sense. However, this is the season for the turning based on remorse and a thoughtful resolution to find a better way. By returning to our roots, nurturing ourselves on what brings us health, we can recover from the past. Thus returning is not an end but a necessary stage, a timely recovery period which enables us to choose a more productive direction for our lives. When spring comes, the passes through the mountains will be safe again, and, like the merchants and the queen, we will do the traveling we are called to do.

Shaughnessy, 114–115, 306–307.
Lynn, 285–292.
Wilhelm/Baynes, 97–100.

25 无妄 ䷘

(wú wàng) Not False

If you are without falsity, then your persistence will be effective. But if someone is not as they should be, you will have disasters. If you have a goal, it will not prosper.

- **Nine in the first place:** If you can proceed without falsity, you will have good fortune.

- **Six in the second place:** If you reap without plowing, or plant without preparing the earth, then you ought to have somewhere else to go.

- **Six in the third place:** An unexpected calamity. Since someone has tethered the ox. A traveler's gain; a city dweller's disaster.

- **Nine in the fourth place:** If you can persist, no blame.

- **Nine in the fifth place:** An unexpected illness: yet without medicine there will be joy.

- **Nine at the top:** When the unexpected prevails, there are disasters. Nothing done under these circumstances will prosper.

Image

Everywhere under the sky, thunder rolls: the image of all beings with the unexpected. Thus the rulers of the past brought prosperity by a timely nurturing of all things.

All things have their seasons, the appropriate times for each to grow, mature, and decline. Wise rulers and managers observe these seasons and work within them, nurturing, weeding, and pruning only at the seasons when these actions are appropriate. For example, pruning is best done in late autumn or winter, when it is least likely to do harm to the health of the tree or shrub. Water is best given when it is most needed, and for some plants need be applied to roots only. Timeliness in actions requires knowledge of the growth cycles of each type of plant, animal, or person. Yet this preparatory knowledge, constantly refined, repays the investment by leading to an unforced long-term flourishing impossible in any other way.

There are times, however, when the world is filled with unexpected events as startling as the crashes of thunder. This hexagram describes such a time. When thunder rolls, animals and humans instinctively stop whatever they are doing. We consider seeking shelter for the duration of the storm. Often we recognize that we are safer where we are than we would be going somewhere else.

In this hexagram thunder is not paired with lightning, so perhaps actual life-threatening danger is not present, only a signal that a change may be coming. While the thunder rolls, it is timely to pause to see what comes next: a downpour and a possible flood, a gentle rain ideal for nurturing new plants, or even continuing drought. Since we do not know yet what the thunder implies, we cannot start any project wisely. To act at a time of such uncertainty is to invite disaster. Yet we should remember that in early China thunder was a welcome sign of possible rain, a scarce resource essential to continuing life.

Shaughnessy, 50–51, 291.
Lynn, 293–298.
Wilhelm/Baynes, 100–103.

26 大畜 ䷙

(dà chù) Great Nurturing

Great nurturing. Persistence is effective. Eating away from home is fortunate. Crossing the great river is effective.

- Nine in the first place: There is danger. It is effective to stop.

- Nine in the second place: The cart loses the fitting which holds it to the axle.

- Nine in the third place: Good horses follow. In difficulties, it is effective to persist. With daily training of your chariot team, a defense. It is effective to have somewhere to go.

- Six in the fourth place: Wood on the horns of the calf. Good fortune from the beginning.

- Six in the fifth place: Remove the boar's tusks. Good fortune.

- Nine at the top: What is the highway of the sky? Success.

Image

Sky within mountain: the image of great abundance. You should learn much from the sayings and deeds of those who preceded you, to nurture your own moral strengths.

What could be more abundant than the skies that lie among mountain peaks? When we have climbed high, we are far more likely to look down at the landscape we came from, even though now it is far away. It is easy to overlook what is most abundantly around us, whether it is the sky at the height of a mountain or good food during a fine harvest. While the overall meaning of this hexagram is very positive, encouraging persistence, moving ahead with a major change, and even eating away from home, many of the lines discuss dangers and ways to avert them.

The moral charge of the image directs your attention to one of the most important methods of self-improvement, learning from what others have said and done. Such examples are as abundant as breezes on a mountaintop, but we often ignore them, especially when we prosper. This hexagram reminds us that we continue to need to learn from the past when we are doing well. Instead of becoming smug, we should pay particular attention to the patterns of others' lives and words, using the abundance of historical examples as both encouragement to do better and as warnings to avoid mistakes. It is only by extending our own experience in this way that we can fully cultivate our own moral strengths at a time when we are doing well.

All lines relate to a need to blunt the effectiveness of a danger. Calves can be trained, so their horns are left intact and simply covered with wood. Boars cannot be trained, however, so their tusks must be removed. Chariots have moving parts that require maintenance and repair. If the pieces which keep the chariot attached to its axle fall off, the cart can no longer be controlled, and it may dump its occupants at any time, even in the midst of battle or a flight from one's enemy. Similarly, horses and charioteers all need constant practice to achieve deftness in their difficult tasks of cooperation, so that they can learn and relearn how to move effectively as one unit.

The broad avenue of the Sky [Heaven] is mentioned much less frequently than the way or road. The pervasive nature of Nature, the naturalness of disparate elements coming together in order to nurture life; that is, to succeed is so obvious that this abundance is usually unnoticed.

Shaughnessy, 56–57, 292.
Lynn, 299–304.
Wilhelm/Baynes, 103–107.

頤 ䷚

(yí) Jaws

Persistence; good fortune. Watching the jaws; seeking food for the mouth.

- **Nine in the first place:** Ignoring your sacred turtle [shell's omens]. Watching our shortened jaws. Misfortune.

- **Six in the second place:** Reversing the jaws. Gnashing at the warp at the north. Going on a campaign would bring misfortune.

- **Six in the third place:** Gnashing the jaws. Persisting brings misfortune. For ten years, don't do it, since no course of action will work out.

- **Six in the fourth place:** Jaws reversed: good fortune. The tiger gazes "dan-dan" (his eyes down], his face "didi" (flute-like). No blame.

- **Six in the fifth place:** Gnashing at the warp [or, knocking the neck]. Persisting where you dwell brings good fortune. You cannot ford the great river now.

- **Nine at the top:** From the jaws, dangers and good fortune. Fording the great river is effective.

Image

Below the mountain, thunder: the image of the jaws. You should use care in your speech and restraint in your eating and drinking.

Thunder here relates to the nourishment that rain brings to growing plants. It is also frightening, indicating a warning related to the ways in which we use our jaws and mouths: in speaking and in eating and drinking, we do well to be sparing and careful in the words and foods we choose to pass through our jaws.

The food and drink we place in our mouths become part of our bodies and affect our feelings and health. Instead of gulping down whatever is available, we need to be cautious and restrained, choosing what we bring between our jaws, and limiting our intake to modest amounts of those foods and drinks that will nourish us best. Similarly, the words and phrases we allow our jaws to form will become part of the social fabric of our lives, enhancing or harming our relationships. Once spoken or written, words cannot be recalled, so we need to choose them with the same care we give to selecting our foods, discarding what is foul or fetid, selecting what is ripe for the time and person, and holding back rash explosions of feeling, which could bring harm to our relationships.

Such restraint in the jaws, holding them still as a mountain at times, is not easy. Yet even tigers manage to keep their mouths

shut when they need to gaze down from their vantage point before beginning their hunt. This hexagram mentions times when
making a major change is wise and times when it is not. Though
one line recognizes a time for moving, most recommend waiting,
and several suggest that starting something major in this situation
would bring about misfortune. This may be a time for restrained
nurturing rather than for decisive action.

Shaughnessy, 66–67, 294–295.
Lynn, 305–311.
Wilhelm/Baynes, 107–111.

(dà guò) Greatly Surpassing

Greatly surpassing. The ridgepole sags. It is good to have a place to go. Success.

- Six in the first place: For your mats, use white rushes. No blame.

- Nine in the second place: The withered poplar sends forth new shoots. An old man attains a wife. No action is unavailing.

- Nine in the third place: The ridgepole sags. Misfortune.

- Nine in the fourth place: The ridgepole sags: good fortune. But with harm, distress.

- Nine in the fifth place: The bitter poplar bears flowers. An older woman gains a noble husband. No blame, no praise.

- Six at the top: Crossing the river in its flood, your head is immersed. Misfortune, but no blame.

Image

A tree submerged in the lake: the image of surpassing.
You should be fearless if you must stand alone, and without resentment if you must withdraw from the world.

This hexagram bears two physical images: one is natural, a tree
submerged by a lake; the other is the ridgepole of the roof of a
house, sagging because the weight of the roof has become too
heavy to support. Both circumstances are potentially catastrophic.
In the case of a tree submerged by a flood, it may recover if the
waters recede quickly, without eroding the earth anchoring its
roots. However, if the tree remains submerged for long, it will die.
And even if the waters recede in time, the tree may have suffered
damage from floating debris or, more seriously, from loosening
of the earth around its roots. To recover from this excess of water,
the tree could well use the care of a gardener, replacing lost soil,
pruning away deadwood, and perhaps some healthy branches so
that the roots have less demand on them, both as anchors and
transmitters of nutrients.

Similarly, a sagging ridgepole is a symptom of a sick house
needing remedial attention. A sudden heavy snowfall could spell
disaster, with the ridgepole breaking under the weight, and the
rafters falling in on the house. With the roof broken, a house cannot endure for long. However, if the ridgepole is supported with
auxiliary timbers or the weight on the roof is lightened, the roof
may endure intact for many years despite being bent out of shape.

In the human realm, the hexagram describes two other ex-
tremes: an older man and an older woman marrying apparently
younger spouses. For the first situation, progeny are likely, which
may be why the *Changes* see this as a positive situation. For the
second, the marriage of an older woman, the oldest layer of the

Changes sees neither praise nor blame; neither good or bad fortune. Later commentaries condemn this situation, but the oldest layer does not.

Only two of the six lines relate to marriage. The image of the hexagram, as a whole, stresses the need for emotional equilibrium in those times when we must stand alone. Such times come to most of us, and need not engender anxiety. While standing alone is never comfortable, and our isolation may be unjust, we are reminded that this situation, like the flood submerging the tree, though overwhelming, may not last long. Once the crisis has passed, we may be able to recover and go on with our lives. In fact, some periods of isolation are normal parts of a principled life. As Confucius wrote, if the Way does not prevail, we should be ashamed to be honored and enriched. There are times when retreat and self-strengthening, even when forced upon us, are precisely what we need most.

Shaughnessy, 132–133, 312.
Lynn, 311–317
Wilhelm/Baynes, 111–114.

29 坎 ䷜

(kǎn) The Abyss

Danger repeated [the abyss]. But if you have sincerity in your heart, success. If you act, you will find rewards.

- **Six in the first place:** Danger repeated. You enter into a dangerous water pit. Misfortune.

- **Nine in the second place:** The pit is deep and dangerous. Seek only small gains.

- **Six in the third place:** The arrival of the repeated danger (multiple pit-traps). Dangers in leaving and in entering the pit trap. Don't!

- **Six in the fourth place:** (this line has to do with the bronze containers used in sacrificial rituals, replacing them with earthenware pots, and with either a wine ladle or angelica coming from a window. The one clear statement is:) In the end, no danger [or blame].

- **Nine in the fifth place:** The pit trap is not full. The hill [or sandbar] is not flat. No danger.

- **Six at the top:** Bound with ropes, placed within prison walls. For three years, not getting out. Misfortune.

Image

Water piled upon water: the image of danger. You should constantly act with moral strength, practicing both teaching and service.

Here the natural image is of abyss piled on abyss, or multiple man-made pit-traps. The danger is that one will fall into one of the many pits. So the advice is primarily cautionary: this is really a very dangerous situation, where misfortune is more probable than success. Nevertheless the hexagram as a whole says good fortune results from sincerity. For truly misfortunate situations, no actions are recommended: presumably the best one can do is to endure. Where there is only danger, however, as in line two, small gains may be possible; presumably large undertakings are not. One may be imprisoned for quite a long time, and be so constrained by conditions and events that the prisoner feels tethered with ropes and surrounded by prison walls of thistles and thorns. However, if it is time for a sacrificial offering and you do not have the usual means for doing them, you may use very humble means, which would be unthinkable in better times.

Remember that change never ends; and that the worst misfortunes end too. This may be a very bitter time, when you have little or no freedom. However, even times as bad as this have their uses. You should still find ways to act with kindness and to practice teaching and service on a very small scale at such times. Remember that the great King Wen was imprisoned for years before his son founded his long-lasting kingdom. Use this time, as he did, to write or to put your thoughts in order, and you will continue to grow even within this temporary captivity.

Shaughnessy, 70–71, 295–296.
Lynn, 317–323.
Wilhelm/Baynes, 114–118.

羅

(lí) The Net

The net. Persistence will bring benefits. Success. Raising a cow: good fortune.

- Nine in the first place: Treading in the old manner. If you respect them, no blame.

- Six in the second place: A yellow net; supreme good fortune.

- Nine in the third place: The net [cast by the] setting sun. Not drumming on the earthenware jar yet singing, then the sigh when the kerchief is worn for mourning. Misfortune.

- Nine in the fourth place: As if an exit; as if an entry. As though burning; as though dying; as though discarded.

- Six in the fifth place: Going out with tears streaming down. Sad enough to sigh. Good fortune.

- **Nine at the top:** The ruler begins a military campaign: joy in decapitating enemies. Capturing those not of our kind. No blame.

Image

Brightness twice makes for cohesion: the image of the net. Thus you should link people of enlightenment throughout the four corners of the earth.

Brightness flaming into brightness above it: this is a kind of cohesion full of flexibility; creative and destructive, it is not restrained. Instead, the crackle and flow of flame upon flame: fire feeding upon its likeness. This is not the way we usually view cohesion or a net. Instead, it is a more fluid and more transformative interaction. The images are a net cast by the setting sun; a cow reared with persistence. Sadness and wailing are associated with good fortune. Singing without beating on clay jars is associated with misfortune.

These are strangely contradictory images. If you have no changing lines, meditate on the types of persistence needed to raise a cow, and the benefits a cow brings to a household, as well as the image of flames above flames. If you have a changing line, meditate on the images there.

Shaughnessy, 134–135, 312–313.
Lynn, 323–328.
Wilhelm/Baynes, 118–121.

31 咸 ䷞

(xián) Reciprocity, Respect

Mutual respect: success. Persistence is effective. To take this woman brings good fortune.

- Six in the first place: Respecting your big toe.

- Six in the second place: Respecting the calf of your leg: misfortune. But staying is fortunate.

- Nine in the third place: Respecting your thigh. Compelled to follow along. Going brings distress.

- Nine in the fourth place: Persistence is fortunate. Remorse disappears. You go back and forth. A friend follows your thoughts.

- Nine in the fifth place: Respecting your spine: no remorse.

- Six at the top: Respect in your cheeks, tongue, and jowls.

Image

Above the mountain, a lake: the image of reciprocity/respect. You should receive others with emptiness. [That is, truly hear them.]

Lakes rarely lie high in the mountains, much less above them. Yet when we find pure water at high elevations, we welcome it and are refreshed. Rain or a spring has found a hollow in which to collect. In order to be truly receptive to others, we need to empty ourselves of expectations and our own ways of seeing, lest they prevent our accurate hearing.

The inner stillness necessary for true receptivity is as hard to reach as the summit of a mountain. The hexagram's progression through the parts of the body suggests that it refers to yoga-like physical exercises designed to bring stillness to the mind through stillness in the body.

Respect and reciprocity are essentially synonyms here. Think on that while stilling your own body, bit by bit, and trying to bring as much stillness to your mind as a clear mountain lake, sheltered by surrounding rocks.

Shaughnessy, 124–125, 309–310.
Lynn, 329–334.
Wilhelm/Baynes, 122–125.

(héng) Duration

Success without blame. Persistence is effective. It is appropriate to have a place to go.

- Six in the first place: Deepening duration. Persistence brings misfortune. Nothing done now would be effective.

- Nine in the second place: Remorse disappears.

- Nine in the third place: Without duration in your moral strength, you will suffer humiliation. Persistence brings troubles.

- Nine in the fourth place: In the fields, neither birds nor beasts.

- Six in the fifth place: Enduring in your moral strength. Persistence. For a wife, good fortune. For a husband, misfortune.

- Six at the top: Shaking constancy; misfortune.

Image

Thunder above the wind: duration. You should take a stand and not change direction.

When thunder rides the wind, it can be heard for many miles. Similarly, when people manage to persist in doing what is right, their influence can be far-reaching. It is not endurance nor longevity alone that is valued here, but persistence in following the truth, in doing what we know is right, in fulfilling our best selves, that moral strength for which "virtue" is a poor translation. It might better be termed what is strongest and most life giving within us, the type of kindness that attracts others with its quiet and radiant receptivity.

Seeking duration alone is not encouraged here, even though persistence is often praised in the *Changes*. There is a contrast between persisting in virtue and all other kinds of duration which are contraindicated. There are also two lines that lack labels about whether they bring good fortune or bad. In one, remorse disappears, which is sometimes the result of a long-lasting commitment. In another, the fields, normally host to birds and animals, are barren of fauna. For a farmer this might be a good situation. But certainly it is odd. There are times when long periods in the same position result in a deadening of the most sprightly aspects of life. While a vegetal existence continues, the full range of life is missing. This is neither the worst situation nor the best.

Shaughnessy, 100–101, 304.
Lynn, 335–340.
Wilhelm/Baynes, 126–129.

33

(dùn) Retreat

Retreat. In minor matters, persistence is effective.

- Six in the first place: At the tail of a retreat, danger. You do not have a place to go.

- Six in the second place: If you apply a yellow leather bridle, none will succeed in breaking away.

- Nine in the third place: Attached to a retreat: there is illness and danger. If you support helpers and intimates: good fortune.

- Nine in the fourth place: Enjoying retreat: for a selfless person, good fortune; for the petty, disaster.

- Nine in the fifth place: Honorable retreat: with persistence, good fortune.

- Nine at the top: Flying retreat: it all works. [lit., there is nothing without benefit]

Image

Beneath the sky, there is a mountain: the image of retreat. You should keep shallow people at a distance, not with hatred but with reserve.

Mountains are great, towering over surrounding lands, even though they cannot reach the sky. Similarly, even the greatest and best people cannot expect a life of continuous progress. For each of us, there are times when we must retreat in the face of stronger forces and distance ourselves from shallow souls.

Recognizing when it is time for a strategic retreat is part of every successful life, for no one pleases everyone, nor should we try to placate shallow minds or uncaring hearts. On the other hand, we must not let our need for distance deteriorate into hatred or expressions of distaste. Such active emotions, though understandable at a time of setback, entangle us further in unproductive wrangling. This is not the time to resist evil or misunderstanding actively, but to subtly withdraw to a safer position.

Times of retreat can be confusing, as they are often occasioned by unexpected defeats or threats of destruction. However, an orderly retreat is not a defeat, but a means of extricating ourselves from real dangers; our primary goal must be self-preservation. In the midst of shock and threats, we may also learn a great deal about others and about ourselves, especially how we appear to others. Although a new direction is as yet unknown, by saving ourselves from an impending disaster, we have given ourselves the time and space to recover, analyze, improve our situation, and seek more favorable circumstances in which to progress.

Shaughnessy, 42–43, 289.
Lynn, 340–345.
Wilhelm/Baynes, 129–132.

34 大壮 ䷡

(dà zhuàng) Great Strength

Great strength. Persistence is effective.

- **Nine in the first place:** Strength in the toes. Going into action will bring misfortune. There will be a return.

- **Nine in the second place:** Persistence brings good fortune.

- **Nine in the third place:** A lesser person uses strength. Someone worthy of leadership does without. Persistence is dangerous. A ram butts against a hedge and gets his horns caught in it.

- **Nine in the fourth place:** Persistence brings good fortune. Regrets vanish. The hedge is broken, the ram's horns free. Strength around the wheels of the cart.

- **Six in the fifth place:** Loss of a ram at Yi. No regrets.

- **Six at the top**: A butting ram gets caught in the hedge. He can neither retreat nor advance. No direction is effective. But after the difficulties, good fortune.

Image

Thunder above the sky: the image of great strength. You should not act without politeness and due process.

Having power over others is like thunder in the sky: it sounds really impressive, but it doesn't last very long. To sustain your position, you need the ongoing support of everyone, especially the ones who seem to keep limiting what you can do. Learn to listen!

The great exegete Kong Yingda wrote: "When your power is at its peak, it is very hard to avoid arrogance." For this reason, good leaders never forget to use good manners: they treat others with respect and deference precisely because they have greater power than most of those they are dealing with. Thus they train themselves to act calmly and to listen to everyone. A duke once received good advice from his driver. Because he was able to hear and heed this advice, which most noblemen would have considered "uppity," he avoided disaster for himself and his country.

True greatness consists of the ability to respect and heed even the most lowly critic; that is, to take everyone as your teacher, your superior in some form of knowledge. If, instead, you get caught up in the trappings of power, which separate you from all but the highest, you will simply immobilize yourself and become ensnared, blinded and rendered ignorant by the sycophants, who will flourish. Delegation and some time alone are both necessary. Autonomy for middle managers and freedom from unimportant details are both necessary. But, if rules of procedure or your own desire for distance result in any actions which could possibly be construed as impolite by anyone, you have created a dangerous situation for yourself. Remember how the strength of the ram made his situation worse when he tried to use his strength to get beyond the boundaries of his field. He lost access to most of his field and gained a most uncomfortable position for his head and body.

Shaughnessy, 88–89, 300–301.
Lynn, 345–350.
Wilhelm/Baynes, 133–136.

晋

(jìn) Advancing

Advancing. The Marquis of Kang was rewarded with many horses and met with the ruler three times in one day.

- Six in the first place: Sometimes advancing, sometimes cut off. With persistence, good fortune. Without sincerity. Yet if lenient, no blame.

- Six in the second place: Now advancing, now in gloom. With persistence, good fortune. Receiving great blessings and prosperity from your Royal Mother.

- Six in the third place: The multitude trusts. Remorse disappears.

- Nine in the fourth place: Advancing like a big rat. With persistence, danger.

- **Six in the fifth place:** Remorse disappears. The arrow is gained without bloodshed. Going is fortunate. Nothing is unprofitable.

- **Nine at the top:** Advance your horns only to attack the city. Danger, good fortune without blame. But persisting brings difficulties.

Image

Light emerges above the earth: the image of advancing. You should enlighten yourself, brightening your moral strengths.

This hexagram describes a time when you are rewarded richly and consulted frequently by those in power. Such a time is likened to dawn, when light seems to emerge from the dark earth and rise above it. In such propitious times, we do well to continue our efforts at self-improvement, and to act with care. While several lines refer to the disappearance of regret, others remind us that increasing danger accompanies a rise in influence and wealth. As Confucius noted, wealth and power gained by immoral means are as sturdy as clouds. While many may trust you now, such a situation rarely lasts long.

Others lines refer to the intermittent nature of influence: sometimes advance, sometimes nearly drowning by reverses. Yielding to greed can be disastrous, however easy it may seem at a time when one is in favor. An early Zhou song cries: "Big rat, big rat, don't eat up my grain!" Avoid using all your available perquisites, and remember that your position is due to the assistance and blessings of others, not your own worth alone. Enjoy the rise, the dawn of recognition, but remember that the light may not be sufficient to see all the pitfalls around you. Be cautious, and continue the self-improvement you began when you had no other means of growth, despite the noise and rewards around you.

Shaughnessy, 138–139, 313–314.
Lynn, 351–357.
Wilhelm/Baynes, 136–139.

36 明夷

(míng yí) Wounded Light

The light is wounded. In difficulties, it is effective to persevere.

- Nine in the first place: Light wounded in flight. You fold your wings. When those worthy of power travel, for three days they do not eat. You have a destination, and a host with words.

- Six in the second place: The light is wounded in the left thigh. You use the strength of a horse to hold yourself aloft. For the great, good fortune.

- Nine in the third place: The light is wounded in the southern hunt. She gains her great leader but cannot be hasty in [promising] constancy.

- Six in the fourth place: The light is wounded in the left of her belly. Spearing the heart of the wounded light, going out of the gates of one's courtyard.

- **Six in the fifth place:** Like the wounded brilliance of the Prince of Ji. Persistence is effective.

- **Six at the top:** Not light but darkness [literally, as little light as the last night of the old moon]. First [light] rises into the sky, afterwards it enters the earth.

Image

The light enters into the earth: the light [of the moon] darkens. Within, cultivate the light; outwardly yield gently. By bearing great difficulties, King Wen used them [to benefit himself and others]. [While imprisoned, he is said to have arranged the Book of Changes].

This hexagram describes the many dark times in history and human lives, when the sources of light seem wounded, struck down as fatally as a bird shot in flight. When the Zhou *Changes* were being assembled, China was recovering from such a time, when the last legitimate Shang king had beset the nation with greed, cruelty, and unpredictability. (They drank copiously from vessels which leached lead into warmed liquors, so there is both textual and archeological evidence for this selfish and irrational behavior.) Two among those who dared to "speak truth to power" were the Prince of Ji, mentioned here, and "King" Wen. The Prince of Ji was a noble advisor to the Shang king. Because he remonstrated with his king, he was thrown into prison. After this evil regime was replaced by the Zhou, the prince was consulted and heeded by the new King Wu of Zhou. The prince then retired, choosing to live in modest circumstances. Words attributed to Prince Ji appear in the Classic of History (*Shujing*). Thus they were memorized by Confucius, his students, and all who studied for the civil service exams which led to government careers. Clearly the prince's advice, shunned at first, was valued later, and he did not suffer lasting harm. He responded well to a dark time.

When light seems to dive below the earth, as pictured here, darkness reigns. At such times, we need to look to the inner light and nourish that. Meanwhile, we may need to yield (or seem to yield) to harsh external conditions for a time. Both Prince Ji and "King" Wen accepted imprisonment under a despotic regime, as Gandhi did. Ji and Wen used their time in jail productively. Ji wrote instructive history. Wen organized divinatory fragments into the *Book of Changes*. Later, their words were used to instruct rulers, managers, and the entire educated elite for millennia. In the long run, they were far more influential than the sycophants who seemed more successful at the Shang court.

Times of pain and suffering do occur and recur, but they also pass and are succeeded by better days, just as a full moon returns after waning.

Shaughnessy, 112–113, 306.
Lynn, 357–362.
Wilhelm/Baynes, 139–142.

37 家人 (jiā rén) Family

Family. It is effective for a woman to persevere.

- Nine in the first place: At the gate, the family. Remorse disappears.

- Six in the second place: Without a place to go. At the center, good food. Persistence brings good fortune.

- Nine in the third place: The family goes "shyow-shyow."* Remorse and danger, but good fortune. Wife and children go "shee-shee."* In the end, distress.

- Six in the fourth place: A prosperous family. Great good fortune.

- Nine in the fifth place: The ruler approaches those with families. Not pity but good fortune.

- Nine at the top: Sincere and awed. In the end, good fortune.

Image

Winds come from the fire: the image of the family. You should use words with substance and acts which endure.

While the effects of wind currents on fires are more visible than the currents produced by flames, our attention here is focused on the latter, as an emblem representing the family. Fire produces heat which rises and causes changes in the motions of the air nearby, particularly in the kind of enclosed space associated with a home. Similarly, the warmth generated by a family also creates motion, both within the group, and among those it impels beyond it, in search of sustenance for the group or countervailing alliances beyond it.

The flickering flames, though anchored by the wood which feeds them, are extraordinarily mobile. In addition, they generate movement in the air surrounding them. It is precisely because of this extreme mobility that we are encouraged to limit ourselves to words which are not light but substantive, and to actions in which we know we can persist. While we may feel warmed and comfortable within our families, it is precisely because these ties last so long that we must be so careful with them, choosing our words with care and selecting actions in which we can persist without doing harm to either ourselves or those near us.

* It is unclear which emotions were associated with these sounds. The first may indicate anger or joy; the second may be happy.

Shaughnessy, 162–163, 321.
Lynn, 363–367.
Wilhelm/Baynes, 143–147.

38 睽 ䷥

(kuí) Double Vision

Double vision. In small matters, good fortune.

- Nine in the first place: Remorse disappears. If you have lost your horse, do not pursue it. It will return by itself. You meet an ugly person. No blame.

- Nine in the second place: You meet a master in a lane. No blame.

- Six in the third place: Meeting with a wagon. Its oxen with crumpled horns. That person bears the branded face and absent nose of a criminal. No beginning, but an end.

- Nine in the fourth place: The cross-eyed loner meets a good person. With mutual trust, there is danger but no blame.

- Six in the fifth place: Regrets vanish. Ascending to the temple: divining, eating, leaving. What blame?

- **Nine at the top:** The cross-eyed loner meets a muddy pig and a cart filled with imps. First, draw the bow. Later, unstring it. If, at dusk, there is no enemy, there will be plenty.

Image

Fire above, water below: the image of double vision. You should act by coordinating, not by taking a separate route.

We rarely see fire above water, whereas the reverse is the productive example of cooking. This is an example of images gone awry, as they do when a person's eyes focus on separate objects instead of providing a clear image of one. Whether eyes are crossed or wall-eyed, the result is the same confusion and inability to accurately judge distances and shapes. Even worse, eventually eyes and mind adjust to this condition by suppressing one of the images. The sufferer from stabismus then seems to see clearly but does not. The crucial ability to sense depth and distance has been lost or skewed.

There may be times in our lives when we seem to see clearly but do not. Great care is necessary at such times. It may be dangerous to make commitments or major decisions while these conditions persist.

Shaughnessy, 142–143, 143–144.
Lynn, 368–374.
Wilhelm/Baynes, 147–150.

39 寨 ䷦

(jiǎn) Impeded

On foot [instead of having wheels]. Effective in the southwest. Not effective in the northeast. It is effective to consult a wise one. Persisting is fortunate.

- Six in the first place: Leaving on foot; coming by chariot.

- Six in the second place: The ruler's officials walk and walk again, but not by reason of themselves.

- Nine in the third place: Going on foot, and coming back.

- Six in the fourth place: Going on foot; coming with connections.

- Nine in the fifth place: When the great walk friends come. You lose.

- Six at the top: Going on foot; coming with a stone. Good fortune. Consulting a great person is effective.

Image

On the mountain, water, the image of impediment. You should turn toward the truth within you and cultivate your moral strengths.

As many thirsty hikers have discovered, it is rare indeed to find water at the top of a mountain. However, when the form of the mountain impedes the flow of water, it may be held in this unusual position. While we usually think of obstruction as being negative, such times of forced inactivity may permit self-nurturing that is impossible in better times, when myriad responsibilities make respites rare, and even the night hours are filled with worries. Such outwardly dreary times, when we lose our accustomed vehicles or powers, force us to slow down and walk. If we can accept such periods calmly, and as transitory, we can use them to advantage. When we are unable to influence others, we may see our own flaws and limits with unusual clarity. However painful this may be, it is useful information, which we do well to absorb and find inner resources to counterbalance, or at least learn to recognize, the flaws such periods bring to light. External obstructions and impediments may in fact provide us with the actual or cognitive leisure to work on ourselves with some of the energies we usually expend on trying to change others. This may be a good time to remember the old joke, "Take my advice, I'm not using it." Try to do some of the good things you recommend to others.

For this hexagram, the comment on the judgment is so helpful, that I have included some of it:

> To be impeded is to be in difficulties. When dangers are before you, to see the danger and be able to stop is wisdom indeed.... Great is the usefulness of a time of impediments!

This statement and the image of pure water surprising a hot and tired climber who has reached the summit of a mountain are fine subjects for meditation during meetings when no one is willing to hear your concerns.

The imagery within the hexagram itself is that of someone who no longer has a vehicle. Instead, she must plod along as others' carts and chariots rush by her, raising dust or mud. It is not a favorable situation in itself, but it can have benefits. Those times when we are forced to slow down and walk force us to be more organized: we must consolidate tasks and cannot afford to forget and leave things behind. We see much more of our surroundings when we walk than when we ride, precisely because we are going more slowly, have less need to be alert for other vehicles, and can actually afford to stop and observe if we wish, without interrupting traffic on the road. While we can carry less, and cannot go so far, we may see and feel more on the way.

Shaughnessy, 76–77, 297.
Lynn, 375–380.
Wilhelm/Baynes, 151–154.

40 解 ䷧

(jiè) Released (Untied)

Released. The southwest works out. If you have no destination, your coming back is fortunate. If you have a destination, good fortune comes in the early morning.

- Six in the first place: No blame.

- Nine in the second place: In the fields, you catch three foxes and gain a yellow arrow. Persistence brings good fortune.

- Six in the third place: Shoulders burdened while riding on a cart. This attracts thieves. Persistence brings distress.
  You need to notice your true circumstances, which are better than you think, and stop clutching everything you have so tightly.

- Nine in the fourth place: Release your thumbs; your friends return.

- Six in the fifth place: Only one worthy of power is released. Good fortune. Return when others are petty.

- **Six at the top:** The duke shoots hawks down from the high wall surrounding the city. Nothing is ineffectual.

Image

Thunder and rain in action: the image of release. You should forgive mistakes and pardon crimes.

This hexagram is about the releasing that must be done by people in high places, those who have more than others. A high position should bring a broader vision and an increased detachment, a lessened need to clutch every advantage you have as a leader, since you have so many. Be more open-handed and honest: you can afford this! The short-run disadvantages may be all too obvious. However, the people you need the most, those with practical experience, will remember that most new systems have bugs, and that no one is perfect. If you can release yourself from your fears of embarrassment, show that you welcome criticism and reward those who point out your mistakes, you will encourage the participation of the most honest and conscientious people in the group and proceed toward workable methods of effective interaction. You should also be tolerant of others' mistakes even when they do something that is clearly wrong.

The natural image for this kind of release from on high is the fecundating (and startling) activities of thunder and rain. Neither is particularly pleasant for anyone caught outside in the downpour, deafened by thunder, and in fear of lightning. However, the land cannot give life to crops and those who use them without plentiful rain, which is usually accompanied by these temporary annoyances. Thunder may feel almost unbearably terrifying, but it is very short-lived, whereas the work of the rain that it brings is quiet, very slow, but absolutely essential to life. So let the criticism come, and let some of your powers remain unused. You won't hear as much flattery, and in the long run this is healthier. Besides, if you have the flexibility to take off your backpack when you have the use of a cart, you will adapt more easily when you lose the cart and must return to walking in the dust of others' carts and shouldering your own burdens. You may well find that your harshest critics become your sincerest friends when you lose the clout that attracted the toadies. And you may be surprised to find your own life far more enjoyable at what others think of as a lower level.

Shaughnessy, 96–97, 303.
Lynn, 380–386.
Wilhelm/Baynes, 154–157.

41 損䷨

(sǔn) Decrease

Decrease. With sincerity, supreme good fortune with no blame. You can persist. It is effective to have a destination. Why use two bowls? You can use fragrant grass. (modest offerings are enough)

- **Nine in the first place:** Stop the service; quickly depart. No blame. You decrease your use of wine toasts.

- **Nine in the second place:** It is effective to persist. To start a campaign brings misfortune. Do not decrease, but increase it.

- **Six in the third place:** If three people walk together, they lose one. If you walk alone, you will gain your friends.

- **Six in the fourth place:** Decreasing your anxiety/illness. If you attend to the endings, there will be happiness. No blame.

- **Six in the fifth place:** Some decrease you by ten strings of turtle shells. You cannot deflect this. Supreme good fortune.

- **Nine at the top:** Not a decrease but an increase, without blame. Persistence brings good fortune. It is effective to have a destination. You attain a helper, but not a home.

Image

Below the mountain, a lake: the image of decrease. You should restrain anger and smother desires.

It is beautiful to see a mountain reflected in a lake at its foot, yet here this is an image of decrease. A lake lying beneath a mountain does not try to climb its heights. This would be absurd. Similarly, in a time of decrease, we need to restrain our anger and desires for things beyond our means, whether these are material objects or prominent acquaintances to which we have become accustomed. Such restraint may not come easily, but try to do it as gracefully as you can. You need to move on now, and you will find that even very modest gifts are sufficient. This decrease is a positive development, the beginning of a time of good fortune.

Shaughnessy, 60–61, 293–294.
Lynn, 387–396.
Wilhelm/Baynes, 158–161.

(yì) Increase

Increase. It is beneficial to have a destination. It is effective to ford the great stream.

- Nine in the first place: It is effective to do a great deed. Great good fortune; no blame.

- Six in the second place: Some success from it: ten double strings of turtle shells. You cannot refuse. The persistence of water brings good fortune. The ruler offers incense to God. Good fortune.

- Six in the third place: Succeeding at it, using service without blame. With a return to the middle ranks, reporting to the duke using a jade slate.

- Six in the fourth place: The middle ranks report to the duke in support. It is beneficial to have a clan and to move the state.

- **Nine in the fifth place:** There is sincerity in a humane heart. No questions; great good fortune. There is sincerity and kind treatment of my moral strengths.

- **Nine at the top:** No one increases it; someone hits it. A heart/mind in place but inconstant. Misfortune.

Image

Wind and thunder: the image of increase. When you see good, you should turn toward it. Where there are mistakes, you should correct them.

Increase here is associated with wind and thunder, a frightening and turbulent image, but less shocking and threatening than lightning. The advice here is of the sort that delighted Confucius. He said, "When I am in a group of only three people walking, I always have two teachers. From the good that I see, I can learn to improve. From the bad, errors that I should correct in myself" (*Analects*). The hexagram is also associated with the support given by the states of Jin and Zheng to Duke Yu of Zhou in the sixth year of his reign, 716 BCE (*Zuo zhuan*, Legge 5:21).

This is a very positive hexagram, encouraging making a major change. As usual, good fortune is accompanied by warnings that doing what is right and correcting errors are also essential.

Shaughnessy, 164–165, 321–322.
Lynn, 396–403.
Wilhelm/Baynes, 162–165.

43 夬

(guài) Resolute

Break-through: Raised into the royal court. A sincere call of "danger!" announced from the city. This is not a time for military force. It is a time to move forward resolutely.

- **Nine in the first place:** Strength in your front toes. This action will not bring victory, only blame.

- **Nine in the second place:** Wary cries at dusk. There military action but no bloodshed.

- **Nine in the third place:** Strength in your cheekbones. Misfortune. Even the best person, going it alone, meets rain and pools of water. There is anger but not blame.

- **Nine in the fourth place:** Thighs without skin: their actions falter. If a ram leads, remorse disappears. Hearing words, but not believing.

- **Nine in the fifth place:** The weeds are broken. With resolution action, walking a middle way, no blame.

- **Six at the top:** Without a cry. In the end, misfortune.

Image

The waters rise up into the sky: the image of resolute action. You should give generously to those beneath you. If you dwell in moral strength, then you will know what to hate.

Water that rises up into the sky is in a position to benefit all beneath it, by giving fructifying rain. Similarly, a good person who has achieved a position of importance and acceptance akin to being a member of a royal court has responsibilities to those less fortunate.

This is a time when you may move ahead with your plans resolutely, so long as you avoid doing harm to others. However, even in good times, when well positioned for action, the *Changes* counsels caution, being receptive to warnings even from unlikely sources, and to the potential for danger. The higher we rise, the more vulnerable we become. Our actions and attitudes become more visible, more displayed and analyzed by others. It is easy to assume that others think our intentions good. In fact, people who feel beneath others often perceive slights and potential harm even when this is the farthest thing from the minds of those who are better off. We may not know of these negative perceptions until we lose our powers, and the vulnerable person turns against us, attacking in what they feel is righteous indignation. A time when resolute progress is possible is a time for greater caution, not less.

Shaughnessy, 120–121, 308.
Lynn, 404–410.
Wilhelm/Baynes, 166–170.

44 姤 ䷫

(gòu) The Royal Bride

The woman is great. Do not grab the woman. A royal bride [was met with great ceremony,] not taken by force.

- Six in the first place: Bound together with a golden spindle. Persevering brings good fortune. Though [you] have a place to go, you face misfortune. With a scrawny piglet to sacrifice, you hesitate.

- Nine in the second place: A fish is in wrappings (conception). No blame. Do not entertain guests.

- Nine in the third place: Buttocks without skin. Her actions halt repeatedly. She hesitates before proceeding. Danger but not much blame.

- Nine in the fourth place: Wrappings but no fish (fetus). True misfortune.

- **Nine in the fifth place:** She protects the babe within, just as a gourd is protected by being wrapped in flexible willow twigs. You hold great beauty within you. If you miscarry, this is Heaven's will.

- **Nine at the top:** The royal bride's horns. Danger but no blame.

Image

Below the sky, a wind: the image of the royal bride. [As gentle and persistent as the wind,] the queen spreads her influence and makes proclamations which reach the four corners of the world.

The influence of a person in a position like that of a royal bride is like that of a wind: above the people, yet below the dictates of the Highest Power. The celebration of her arrival is impressive, and her eventual influence may be profound. Despite the great hopes raised at her marriage, her initial position is tenuous, since it is based on the hope for a son not yet conceived.

Just as the winds sweep over the whole world, her influence may transform her new country if her son becomes the next ruler. However, first she must conceive and bear a healthy son. Therefore most of the lines refer to conception and the stages of pregnancy, and to the risks surrounding the gestation period. The image describes the gentle power of the wind, which can shape a landscape if it continues to blow in the same direction for many years.

This hexagram may celebrate the royal marriage that resulted in the birth of the founder of the Zhou dynasty, King Wu. According to the Classic of Poetry (*Shijing*), his father honored the princess who was his bride by going to meet her. In emulation of this example, later kings sent their highest officials to welcome a royal bride before she reached her new home. For a description of another ceremonious greeting of a royal bride, see *Shijing* 261.

Shaughnessy, 52–53, 291–292.
Lynn, 410–416.
Wilhelm/Baynes, 170–174.

45 萃 (cuì) Gathered Together

Gathered together. Success. The ruler enters the temple. It is effective to meet with a great person. Success. It is effective to persist. Sacrificing a great ox brings good fortune. It is effective to have a place to go.

- Six in the first place: If there is sincerity, but not to the end, then there is sometimes chaos, sometimes gathering together. As if crying out, in one room. If there is laughter without bloodshed, then action is without blame.

- Six in the second place: With a bow, good fortune without blame. If you are sincere, then doing the spring sacrifice is effective.

- Six in the third place: Like gathering, like crying. Inaction is effective. Going is blameless, misfortunes small.

- Nine in the fourth place: Great good fortune, without blame.

- **Nine in the fifth place:** Gatherings together take place. No blame, no trust. With enduring persistence, remorse disappears.

- **Six at the top:** Weeping and crying, but no blame.

Image

A lake above the earth, the image of massing together. You should gather your weapons together to cope with the unexpected.

As lake levels rise above the contours of the land, individual ponds and streams merge into larger and larger expanses of water. This natural occurrence is analogous to the way in which a leader gradually builds support, or a warrior prepares by assembling all weapons. Great changes are possible only when a leader has assembled masses of supporters, and when they cohere as completely as droplets do in making a lake.

Although water was often scarce in early China, here it is almost too plentiful. A clear statement of success describing the situation as a whole is coupled with a warning that the future is unpredictable, so that now is the time to make sure your strengths are mustered and in order, your assets available for any unforeseen difficulty.

Shaughnessy, 122–123, 308–309.
Lynn, 417–423.
Wilhelm/Baynes, 174–177.

46 升 ䷭

(shēng) Pushing Upwards

Pushing upwards: great success. Consult a great one now, to be without anxiety. Proceeding to the south brings good fortune.

- Six in the first place: Advancing upwards. Great good fortune.

- Nine in the second place: If you are sincere, then your making the summer sacrifice is effective. No blame.

- Nine in the third place: Going up to the empty city.

- Six in the fourth place: The ruler made an offering on Mount Qi. Good fortune without blame.

- Six in the fifth place: Persistence brings good fortune, pushing upwards in stages.

- Six at the top: Pushing upwards in the darkness just before dawn. An unswerving persistence is effective.

Image

Within the earth a tree grows: the image of pushing upwards. You should adhere to moral strength, piling up
small things in order to attain great heights.

A tree is born within the earth, with the sprouting of a seed. As it
grows, it pushes the earth aside as it stretches and grows towards
the water and sun it needs to live. Trees can grow in rich or stony
soil and attain sturdy trunks and branches that will live many decades, even for centuries. But their growth is so slow that at times
it is barely discernible, especially when compared to the growth
of short-lived plants.

For human beings also, the kind of growth that leads to enduring strength is measured and slow. The daily increment may
be so small that at times it seems as if no progress is being made.
For this reason, it is helpful to maintain rituals, such as regularly
repeated visits with wise people. Reunions or annual gatherings of
family or friends may seem pointless, but in fact they allow us to
see how far those we know best have come since we last saw them.
And they, in turn, may help us see our current state of progress
more clearly. Some stages may seem hollow gains, like climbing
to a city on a hill only to find that it is uninhabited. Taking part
in rituals can help us assuage our anxieties and move beyond
them, as we unite ourselves with others and with unseen forces
in performing them.

In the long life of a tree there are many winters, when visible
growth above ground pauses, and for months the tree may look
dead. But beneath the snow and earth the roots continue to grow,
deepening the tree's anchor to the ground, preparing it for times
of drought, when water can only be found at great depth.

During winter, remember spring and Goethe's poem about
trees: now only sticks, these trees will one day give shade and fruit,

as will we flourish if only we persist. As Xunzi said, even a lame turtle can reach her goal, if she just keeps putting one foot ahead of the other. In a fast-paced world, it can be hard to remember how long really solid growth takes. This hexagram reminds us of the tenacity of trees, the usefulness of sequential small steps and ritual celebratory gatherings. Giving to others with less helps us remember how many gifts we have; helping others learn can help us see how much we have learned.

Even seemingly impossible goals, like transforming ourselves into sages, are possible if we just keep piling up good deeds. Eventually, we will reach our goals. See Xunzi, chapters 1 and 2.

Shaughnessy, 116–117, 307.
Lynn, 423–428.
Wilhelm/Baynes, 178–181.

(kùn) Exhaustion

Exhaustion. Good fortune with persistence. For a great one, good fortune without calamities, even though when you speak, others do not believe you.

- Six in the first place: Buttocks exhausted, at the roots of a tree. As you enter a shadowy valley, for three years you see no one.

- Nine in the second place: Exhausted with food and drink. When the ceremonial red garment arrives, it is effective to wear it when offering the ritual sacrifice. To start a campaign leads to misfortune but no blame.

- Six in the third place: Exhausted amid rocks, you grasp a thorny branch. When you enter your home, you do not see your wife. Misfortune.

- Nine in the fourth place: It comes slowly, slowly, exhausted by a metal chariot. Humiliation that ends.

- **Nine in the fifth place:** [You have received the harsh punishment of having your] nose or leg cut off. Oppressed while wearing a red ceremonial garment. Then slowly there is joy. Making the sacrifice is effective.

- **Six at the top:** Held back by [entangling] vines and grass. Anxious and perplexed. Think of moving with regret. Though you will have regrets, persisting will bring good fortune.

Image

A marsh with its water beneath it, the image of exhaustion. You may need to sacrifice your life if only this will achieve your goals.

When a marsh or lake loses its water, it loses its vitality, and many of the living things depending on it die. The drying hole stinks of decaying fish and plants. If the dryness continues, the lake eventually loses its identity as a lake, distinct from the land. There are times when we must face complete exhaustion, a lack of the most basic necessities of life. Achieving a cherished goal may be costly, even to the extent that we sacrifice our health and our lives. Going on beyond what is sustainable should only be done for the noblest of goals, since it may preclude all that continued life may promise. Still, there are times and goals deserving of such sacrifices. Remember that exhaustion, like the other stages of change, does not last forever.

Shaughnessy, 126–127, 310–311.
Lynn, 428–437.
Wilhelm/Baynes, 181–184.

(jǐng) The Well

The well. Move the city but do not move the well. No loss, no gain: going to and coming from the well. But if it dries up, the rope is not yet there, or the bucket is damaged, misfortune.

- Six in the first place: The well is muddy, no drinking from it. An old well, without birds.

- Nine in the second place: In the well's depths, shooting at little fish. The bucket leaks.

- Nine in the third place: The well is repaired but its water is not drunk. My heart is sad. It can be used and drunk if the ruler is enlightened and bestows his good fortune on others.

- Six in the fourth place: The well is repaired; no troubles.

- Nine in the fifth place: The well has cold spring water. Drink it.

- **Six at the top**: You take from the well without covering it. If you are sincere, great good fortune.

Image

Above wood, there is water: the image of the well. You should reward others and all should encourage each other.

This character is a picture of the wood used to make the crosspieces at the top of a well. It is these pieces of wood which enable us to raise the water beneath us to our own level. This represents the human apparatus that enables people to reach and share the resources they need. First, one must locate reliable springs, even those well below the level of the earth. Then the well must be excavated, the hole preserved with bricked walls, the wooden frame provided at the top, with the rope and bucket or pot to draw the water up.

Such wellsprings are so important that we cannot live far from them. We may move our houses, even our cities, but we cannot eliminate our need for water. Therefore, we must safeguard wells and maintain them. If they are muddy, this must be fixed by digging deeper or replacing bricks that have fallen and allowed earth to sift down into the water. If the rope or bucket is broken, it must be mended or replaced. An enlightened leader avoids calamities by making sure all these components are kept in good working order, and sees that access to the well is shared, not locked down with a lid, which excludes some.

The spring that furnishes water for a well is inexhaustible, but the human apparatus to reach the water is not. Bricks, ropes, and water pots break; buckets develop leaks; the wooden surrounding frames decay. All must be maintained in order to avoid disasters as dire as depriving an entire city of its water. Instead of neglecting the reliable sources of our sustenance, whether they are water, shelter, or relationships, we need to remember to maintain them before they are muddied or broken. Enlightened leaders minimize the probability of disasters by remaining conscious of the wellsprings of life for the group they serve even when they seem so reliable as to be easily forgotten. Individuals also need to notice what sustains them, both bodily and emotionally, to maintain these lifelines even if they seem quite humble and unimportant. What are the things that enable you to live? Who are the people who can be entrusted with caring for the basics that really matter? If your bodily needs are met, if you have clean water to drink, you are among the fortunate few in this world. So often we do not notice what is most valuable to us until we lose it. Much of wisdom consists of being mindful of these basics—physical, economic, social, and psychic.

Shaughnessy, 84–85, 299–300.
Lynn, 438–443.
Wilhelm/Baynes, 185–188.

(gé) Molting (Shedding)

Molting. The day after the zenith, return. Supreme success. Persistence is effective. Remorse disappears.

- **Nine in the first place:** Tie it with leather from a yellow cow.

- **Six in the second place:** The day after the zenith, shed it. Beginning a campaign brings good fortune, without blame.

- **Nine in the third place:** Attacking brings misfortune. Persistence brings danger. Shedding words, calculating three times. Return.

- **Nine in the fourth place:** Remorse disappears. If there is sincerity, a change in the mandate brings good fortune.

- **Nine in the fifth place:** A great person, a tiger changing. Not yet a prediction, but a return.

- **Six at the top:** One worthy of power, a leopard changing. A petty person, a facial change. If you start a campaign, misfortune. If you stay and persist, good fortune.
  This may mean that a great and good person changes as rarely as a leopard changes its spots, whereas a shallow person vacillates as easily as facial expressions change. Thus persistence is valued far higher than frequent changes.

Image

Within the marsh there are flames: the image of molting. Thus you should illuminate the seasons by bringing order to the calendar.

Shedding feathers or skin is a normal and essential part of growth in many animals. This timely discard of bodily debris is likened to a wildfire sweeping through a marsh and to calendrical reforms and reforms of government. (The character for molting can also be translated as *revolution*.)

In all these cases, we may first notice the discarding of the outgrown skin or the terrible destructiveness of a fire as it consumes years of old growth and any animals unable to escape. Such times are so shocking that they should come rarely and only when the times are ripe; that is, after the organism or institution has passed its zenith and can grow no more in its current form. During these times we need to keep our focus on the very long view, thinking in terms of many years of past experience and future goals, just as astronomers do on those rare occasions when they readjust the calendar so that it fits the actual seasonal events more closely. The Chinese used intercalary months occasionally for this purpose.

The discarding of dead matter during a period of shedding may be as gentle as a cat's grooming or as violent as a civil war. Such periods should inspire us to a greater recognition of the many kinds of timeliness and a commitment to finding ways for more orderly and less destructive movement through change, such as those provided by a sound constitution or well planned new growth. In any case, even in the midst of the fiery destruction we should remember that this shedding is a normal and necessary preparation for new life. If the snake does not shed its skin, it cannot grow. If the old feathers do not fall, the new ones cannot grow in to replace them. This less visible part of the molting process is the reason for the discards: new growth is coming, and needs room. We cannot cling to every bit of debris we create and still move ahead.

Since the growing season in north China is very short, one of the oldest responsibilities of government there was the construction of an accurate calendar and instruction to farmers on when to plant their crops. This required accurate records of astronomical and weather phenomena over hundreds of years as well as timely adjustments to ensure that the humanly designated seasons and months remained synchronized with the actual progression of the seasons. In the midst of the rapid destruction accompanying radical governmental change, it is not always easy either to have access to all this data or to use it with the care necessary for such essential pattern recognition and creation of a usable pattern within which to act. In the midst of the flames, our first thought is of flight and self-preservation. Yet a time of shedding is precisely when we most need to do this. Anyone who has emptied their home before moving or after the death of a loved one will understand this.

Shaughnessy, 128–129, 311.
Lynn, 444–451.
Wilhelm/Baynes, 189–192.

(dĭng) The Cauldron

The cauldron. Success from the beginning.

- Six in the first place: The cauldron is filled to the foot. It is well to expel the negative and to take a partner for the sake of the child. No blame.

- Nine in the second place: The cauldron is filled. While my enemies are ill, they cannot limit me. Good fortune.

- Nine in the third place: The loops atop the cauldron [lit., its ears] are cut, so moving it is difficult and the [delectable] pheasant dish inside cannot be eaten. Widespread rain reduces regrets. In the end, good fortune.

- Nine in the fourth place: The cauldron has a broken leg, overturning the duke's food. Punished by [confinement to a single] room. Misfortune.

- Six in the fifth place: The cauldron has brass loops and a metal handle [to slip through them.] Persistence is effective.

- **Nine at the top:** A cauldron with a jade handle [to slip through the loops.] Great good fortune. Nothing is ineffective.

Image

Above the wood there is fire: the image of the cauldron. You should make your position correct in order to clarify your destiny.

We put wood into the flames to feed the fire which rises to cook our food. In a similar manner, we put food into cauldrons (pots and pans) in order to cook it, then share it with others. So the image here is that of a *ding*, an ancient Chinese cooking pot with legs, which could be set directly among the flames without any additional tools such as a stove or separate tripod. The focus here is on the process of cooking, and on the vessel that makes it possible to bring fire and food into close proximity for this purpose. In addition to the primordial meaning of all gathering around the cooking fire or hearth, this hexagram has the additional weight of the powerful religious and political rituals that took place around these bronze cauldrons. During these rites, which carried much greater weight than written laws at that time, the animals, which had been sacrificed to the Lord on High and other spirits often in conjunction with a series of divinations using ox scapulae, were used to make stews which, in turn, were cooked as offerings. The king then shared these precious viands with those he had chosen as his closest and most trusted followers, to whom he also granted fiefs and control of them.

On the whole, the situation symbolized by the cauldron and the wood consumed by the flames is a positive one, presaging success. The act of cooking brings together the fruits of the interactions of nature and humans; that is, good ingredients with the expertise and tools needed to make the most of these ingredients. At the same time, it brings people together to share the provender, an implicit statement of mutual trust, sharing of our essentials with people we can trust not to poison them or to grab them from us. Altogether, this is a complex image of many forces, natural and human, brought together to provide nourishment and community.

Shaughnessy, 148–149, 317.
Lynn, 451–459.
Wilhelm/Baynes, 193–197.

51 震䷲

(zhèn) Thunder

Thunder comes, "xi, xi" shouts. Laughing words: "ya, ya!" The thunder sets all a-tremble for seventeen* miles, without a spill from ladle or cup [used at the sacrifice].

- Nine in the first place: Thunder comes, with renewal, "hu, hu." After it, laughing words, "ya, ya!" Good fortune.

- Six in the second place: Thunder comes with danger. "Yi!" you lose your money [lit., cowry shells]. Ascend the nine peaks [to sacrifice], and do not pursue it. After seven days, you will get it.

- Six in the third place: Thunder threatens, "Su, su." Thunder acts without disasters.

- Nine in the fourth place: After the thunder, mud.

- Six in the fifth place: Thunder comes and goes: danger. "Yi!" no loss, but service [to give].

- **Six at the top**: Thunder sounds: "suo, suo." Fear and trembling, then looking all about. If you start a campaign now, misfortune. Lightning does not strike your own body, but it reaches your neighbor. No blame. In marriage, there are words.

Image

Thunder and lightning doubled: the image of thunder. You should use your fears and anxieties to examine and cultivate yourself.

Thunder and lightning are terrifying. The loud noises travel huge distances quickly; the lightning is a real danger. You may be in the middle of a very serious and delicate undertaking, such as one of the great political-religious rituals of ancient China, when the shocking occurrence happens. But even in times as terrifying as this, it is important to keep steady hands and heart.

Times of terror and tumult terrify most of us, awing us with the uncontrollable powers of nature, which are far beyond our ability to predict or control them. But we can control our reactions to them, and steady ourselves physically and psychically, using times of terror to see others and ourselves more clearly, and rectifying the weaknesses they lay bare. We cannot stop the thunder or the fear it inspires, but we can learn to steady our hands during the storms, to complete our tasks, and to steady our hearts by learning to laugh and share words with others. Storms pass, they may come again. But we can learn how to improve our thoughts and feelings by observing and improving our behaviors in crisis.

* 100 *li*, one *li* being 890 feet. Approximate.

Shaughnessy, 86–87, 300.
Lynn, 460–466
Wilhelm/Baynes, 197–200.

(gèn) Stillness

Still your back, don't move your body. You go into your courtyard without seeing others. No blame.

- **Six in the first place:** Still your feet. No blame. Long-lasting persistence is effective.

- **Six in the second place:** Still your calves, do not raise your legs. Your heart is unhappy.

- **Nine in the third place:** Still your midsection; scratch your spine. In danger of burning the heart. (or suffocating it with smoke)

- **Six in the fourth place:** Still your torso. No blame.

- **Six in the fifth place:** Still your cheeks. You speak in order. Regrets disappear.

- **Nine at the top:** Honest and still. Good fortune.

Image

Linked mountains: the image of stillness. You should be-
ware if you depart from your own place.

The early Chinese lived among chains of mountains and must
have been impressed by their solidity and immobility. They are
very much rooted in and of the earth, heavy, and immovable.

In some situations, it is best to be still, to straighten your back,
become aware of your location, and remain motionless. In periods
of such stillness, we may also learn to still our minds and hearts,
and to view the world with equanimity rather than through a
storm of emotions.

This hexagram may refer to yoga-like physical postures and
exercises used in early China, before any known contact with In-
dian culture. The word *stillness* is a homonym for *root*, the title
used in the Mawangdui text. In a still posture, one endeavors to
root oneself in place, to feel a part of where one is at that moment, as a preparation for detaching one's mind from the many
places and problems tumbling through it. By focusing on one
place, we are able to pay less attention to other places. We can
then keep moving focus toward a stillness that moves from the
body (and its involuntary twitches) to the mind and heart (and
their involuntary twists and worries). This hexagram does not
discuss what we may gain from stillness, only the stillness itself.
And it reminds us, as do other hexagrams, that periods of stillness
are part of the grand process of change, which rarely moves at a
smooth, even pace. Even the busiest people may find that a short
period of stillness, a redirection of focus, enables them to return
to work refreshed and with greater clarity. To be still and aware
of one's place is not a permanent condition, but it is one that can
be beneficial for anyone.

Shaughnessy, 54–55, 292.
Lynn, 466–472.
Wilhelm/Baynes, 200–201.

(jiàn) Gradual Progress

Gradual progress. A woman reaches her marital home. Good fortune. Persistence is effective.

- Six in the first place: The wild geese reach the edge of deep waters. Their little one is endangered. There is talk, but no blame.

- Six in the second place: The wild geese reach a slope where food and good drink are ample. Good fortune.

- Nine in the third place: The wild geese reach the plateau. The husband, sent on a campaign, will not return. The wife is pregnant but does not give birth. Misfortunes. [Still,] resisting thieves is effective.

- Six in the fourth place: The wild geese reach the trees. Someone straightens their rafters [so that they no longer sag]. No blame.

- **Nine in the fifth place:** The wild geese reach the hill. For three years, the wife does not conceive a child. In the end, no one wins. [Nevertheless,] good fortune.

- **Nine at the top:** The wild geese attain the plateau. Their feathers may be used as emblems. Good fortune.

Image

Above the mountain, a tree: the image of gradual progress. You should find places for the worthy and virtuous, and thus bring goodness to prevailing customs.

A tree on a hill or mountain may itself be stunted, but it stands taller than trees planted on lower surfaces. We need to be mindful of our resting places and true homes and how they sustain us in our journeys through our lives. Just as wild geese in migration must rest on their way, we too need to pause as we make progress, to rest, feed our bodies and souls, and reestablish closer communications with those who are flying with us. It makes no sense to try to travel thousands of miles without regular respites. We need to come to earth and refuel. But we also need to be aware of the different natures of our landing spots. Food and rest are more safely acquired on land, so it is wise to take a rest before crossing a deep chasm.

The human image here is of a bride who has found her true home but has not yet produced the son her husband's family wants from her. Her position is extremely insecure, since her name will not be recorded in the ancestral tablets of her marital family until she does produce a son. Virtually all adult women derived their powers through the successes of their adult sons. Another form of insecurity comes from outside the family. If the nation goes to war, and sends the husband into battle, it is unlikely that her husband will ever return.

Both the childless wife and the migrating goose are in transit; they have not yet reached their safe havens. Nevertheless, both need to alight and take what comfort, sustenance, and rest they can while en route. Temporary havens are not to be despised; they are essential to successful migration.

When making analogies with a wife who is either childless or loses her husband to war, it is important to remember that in early China women remarried without incurring the social stigma typical of the last imperial dynasties. In addition, some childless elite women adopted children of their husbands' concubines or lesser wives and attained great power in this way. This was not the common or safest method of advancement for a woman, but it was done. In addition, women served functions other than childbearing. One Shang queen led several successful military campaigns, several advised on the significance of divinations, and in the Han dynasty at least one woman scholar spent most of her life teaching and writing history as an imperial official. These particular women did have children (and presumably child care), and an independent economic existence for an unmarried woman was still an extreme rarity, if it occurred at all. So it is important to remember that the childless woman in this hexagram is a symbol, just as the migrating goose is, not a reference to a particular childless woman in our modern world. Thus this image could represent a trainee in a company or a student in a school, an executive seeking to prove herself with demonstrable bottom line success. In all these cases, there are needed spots for respites from the struggle for progress. And in all these cases, the best sort of person seeks a home both for herself and her most worthwhile qualities and for others of worth and virtue, as a means of being part of a general progress towards a better society. Even as we are in transit, we should try to move toward these goals wherever we alight, even if only for a while.

Shaughnessy, 156–157, 319–320.
Lynn, 473–479.
Wilhelm/Baynes, 204–208.

54 歸妹 ䷵

(guī mèi) Coming Home

A woman enters her marital home. Starting a campaign: misfortune. Not leaving is effective.

- Nine in the first place: A woman comes to her new family as though a younger sister. The lame can walk. With such a start, good fortune.

- Nine in the second place: The one-eyed can see. For a person in the shadows, persistence is effective.

- Six in the third place: Coming home as though low in rank [literally, a concubine]. Return for a maiden marrying as though a younger sister.

- Nine in the fourth place: The marriage is postponed. The delay is timely.

- Six in the fifth place: Lord Yi sent a maiden [his daughter?] in marriage, with lordly sleeves less impressive than those of a younger sister. After several months, hope for good fortune.

- **Six at the top:** A woman holds a basket without fruit. A man stabs a sheep, but no blood. Not acting is effective.

Image

Thunder over the lake: the image of a woman coming home. Thus you should understand things that wear out in the context of the eternity of the soul.

Thunder sounds dangerous, but it presages the arrival of the rain bringing the water essential to the life of the lake. When the thunder brings the rain, the lake will be filled, most fully itself.

The hexagram describes the moment when a newly married bride reaches the home where she will belong for the rest of her life. While this should be the most joyous and auspicious moment of her life, such a moment also arouses justifiable fears, since her future will depend on the relationships she builds with two complete strangers: her husband and her mother-in-law.

For the mother of the groom, this may be the first time she has outranked anyone in the household, and finally has made the transition out of the effective servitude of a new bride herself. Since she has mothered an adult son, she cannot be divorced. Even if her husband's eyes (and heart) wander, any woman he chooses will be only a concubine, never the legal wife and controller of the household, which she has become.

For many older women in families without servants, their son's bride was the first subordinate they had ever had. It was all too common for the older woman to remember her own ill-treatment at the hands of her mother-in-law and the decades of silently endured suffering, and to inflict the remembered pain on the new bride. The bride had no legal recourse if she was mistreated. And on her arrival, she had no allies within the household.

This signifies the beginning of what may be a fulfilled and fulfilling life, which gives her a home, food and security for the rest of her life. But this is usually her only chance at success as a woman, so the fears at first may seem even greater than her hopes. Like hexagram 53, this applies not only to a bride, but to a new career, undertaking, or phase.

Shaughnessy, 94–95, 302–303.
Lynn, 480–487.
Wilhelm/Baynes, 208–212.

(fēng) Abundance

Abundance—success. The ruler approaches you. Have no fears: be like the sun at noon.

- Nine in the first place: Meeting your consort and leader, only for ten days. No blame. If you go, there are rewards.

- Six in the second place: Abundant the curtains. At noon, you see the Big Dipper. In going, gaining suspicion in haste; in returning, these vanish. Good fortune.

- Nine in the third place: Your hedge is abundant. At noon, you see small stars. You break your right arm. No blame.

- Nine in the fourth place: Your curtains are abundant. At noon, you see the Big Dipper. Meeting an alien leader. Good fortune.

- Six in the fifth place: With the coming of the light, there are celebrations and praise: good fortune.

- **Six at the top:** Abundant your rooms, screened your house. Watching the window. Vacant, without others. For three years unseen. Misfortune.

Image

Thunder and lightning come together: the image of abundance. This is how you should decide lawsuits and apply punishments.

The two natural images associated with abundance seem very different. The older, in the hexagram itself, is of the sun at noon, filling the world with light. It is a natural symbol of abundance in its height and dominant position. Yet its usage as a symbol of abundance reminds us that such periods, though real, are transitory. The sun does not stay its course, no matter how slow it may seem in the middle of the day. This is a time to enjoy the present and the illustrious colleagues abundance brings, and to spread one's own light widely. Most of the lines are positive, though a number describe rather odd astronomical phenomena: seeing stars at noon, through the use of curtains or hedges.

The image of thunder and lightning together also emphasizes the transitory nature of abundance, as neither is a lasting part of nature as are earth, sky and mountains. At the peak of one's power, one must make difficult decisions and mete out punishments as well as rewards. How is this like thunder and lightning? Thunder and lightning are loud and shocking, heard far away. Yet they promise life-giving rain. Appropriate punishments should be similar: public, known and clear to all, with reverberations throughout the land, in order to warn others of the real danger of committing crimes. Yet, like thunder and lightning, times of punishment must pass, leaving almost everyone unscathed. They should be followed by generosity as thorough as rain.

Shaughnessy, 98–99, 303–304.
Lynn, 487–493.
Wilhelm/Baynes, 213–216.

旌 56 ䷷

(lǚ) The Wanderer

The wanderer, success in what is small. The wanderer's constancy brings good fortune.

- Six in the first place: A wanderer trivial and humble; this is what gains a fire for you.

- Six in the second place: The wanderer stops at an inn. Cherishing what you have collected, you attain the constancy of a young servant.

- Nine in the third place: The wanderer burns her lodging, and loses her servant boy. Here persistence is dangerous.

- Nine in the fourth place: The wanderer at a stopping point. Though I obtain goods and axe, my heart is not glad.

- Six in the fifth place: Shooting a pheasant, losing one arrow. In winter, you receive a promotion.

- **Nine at the top:** The bird burns her nest. The traveler first laughs, then weeps aloud. Losing the ox at Yi. Misfortune.

Image

Above the mountain, there is fire: the image of the wanderer. You should use clarity and precision when punishing, and not let litigation continue.

When there is fire upon a mountain, its blaze lights up the land around it. The blaze passes swiftly across the tops of trees or shrubs. In the same way, the circumstances in a case should be fully illumined and understood before any punishments are applied, and the process of litigation should also proceed swiftly. Justice delayed is justice denied and enmity spread. At the same time, great care must be taken that facts and contexts are seen clearly, lest greater injustice be done.

How does this relate to the wanderer? Like the fire on the mountain, a traveler does not tarry long in any one place. We are more vulnerable when on the road, away from our homes and families, and among people who may misunderstand our motives or mistrust us simply because we are strangers. Losses of lodgings, supporters, or of possessions hit more heavily when we are traveling, since we have fewer available resources and are less trusted because we do not have a recognized place in the foreign community. In these circumstances, we do well to remain polite at all times, receptive to clues about others' expectations or customs, and careful not to offend. We must not assume that our values are shared, and we cannot afford to seem to ridicule or belittle those around us. We do well to have ample financial resources, so that we can make treating us well worthwhile for these strangers.

For some people, it may be possible to live a life without ever moving or traveling beyond one's home, and thus to avoid this type of vulnerability. But for most of us, there are recurrent periods when we are the stranger, the visitor, the new person in town. With wealth and consideration, these can be comfortable and pleasant periods, but we are never as well protected as we are on our home turf, where our claims to power, our roles interacting with others, are accepted and well known. This hexagram reminds us of the inherent vulnerability of the traveler, the stranger. In addition to warning us to take care on our wanderings, it should remind us to offer kindness and understanding to wanderers we encounter. Some of the most unprepossessing strangers, arriving without any introductions, have brought blessings to those who treated them as their guests. We may learn much from the wanderers.

A further note: In early China, fire was used to clear mountainous land and prepare it for cultivation or easier access by humans. So for them it was a civilizing, fructifying act, not one of long-term destruction. In the same way, in being wanderers (or pilgrims), we must leave behind many ties and almost all physical possessions. But by acceding to this emptiness and vulnerability, we open ourselves to new worlds, some of which may be far more fruitful for us than our current homes.

Shaughnessy, 140–141, 314.
Lynn, 494–500.
Wilhelm/Baynes, 216–219.

巽 ䷸

(xùn) Calculation, Choosing

Calculation, compliance: In what is small, success. It is effective to have a destination and to meet with a great one.

- Six in the first place: Advance and retreat: this is the constant for a warrior.

- Nine in the second place: Choosing to be under the bed: usage which makes witches seem indignant. Good fortune without blame.

- Nine in the third place: Repetitious calculations: trouble.

- Six in the fourth place: Regrets disappear. [Hunting, you catch three kinds of game.]

- Nine in the fifth place: Persisting: good fortune. Regrets disappear. Nothing is ineffectual. Nothing at first but you have it in the end. Before the *geng* day, three days. After the *geng* day, three days. Then good fortune.

- **Nine at the top**: Divining under a bed, you lose your sacred axe. Persistence brings misfortune.

Image

Wind follows wind: the image called compliance or calculation. You should fulfill your destiny by doing what you are called to do.

The various translations for the name of this hexagram (calculation, compliance, divining) are all similar in that they refer to a time when we seek to comply with what is right by consulting the oracle through a method of divination which uses numbers. The insights derived in this way may be as hard to grasp as the wind, as subtle as a gentle breeze. Yet they can help to lead us in the direction we should go if we listen with courage rather than cringing, and if we persist in moving toward this direction over time.

Another way to put this is: Wind follows wind: this is the image of true compliance. You should reiterate what you are called to do, then do it. Though air is invisible and winds are intermittent, few forces are stronger over time. A continuing wind can bend giant trees, erode earth and stone, shape landscapes and vegetation. To accomplish your greatest task, the work you are truly called to do, you must do many small things, travel, seek and heed advice, again and again. As you do this, do not look for great leaps forward, but think of one wind following another; that is, pushing softly again and again. This can be hard to do. When progress seems to be leading into danger or is blocked by more pressing demands, you may feel like hiding under your bed, and doing nothing but the bare essentials. But such slavish compliance with the more obvious powers of your world often leads in the end to regrets and personal promise unfulfilled. This is not what you are called to do. While remaining prudent, we need to remember the immense power of persistent winds. Listen to the still small voice within you, especially when a careful process of divination, consultation, and planning has led to a recognition of something you are called to do. Find another small step toward that goal and do it, and keep repeating this process. If you define your goal carefully, and persist in it, you will inevitably make progress towards it.

All this is posited on the belief that each of us, being unique, is called to do something that no one else can do as well. Identifying this goal may seem to take forever; achieving it even longer! But thoughtful, balanced seeking, without repeated seeking for a different answer, can usually help us discern whether a given action is likely to move us in the right direction or not. Repeating such steps is worthwhile, even if each one seems as small and as evanescent in effect as a puff of wind. As Xunzi said, "Achievement consists of never giving up."

Shaughnessy, 150–151, 317–318.
Lynn, 501–506.
Wilhelm/Baynes, 220–222.

58 (duì) Joy

Joy. Success. Moderate persistence is effective.

- Nine in the first place: Harmonious joy; good fortune.

- Nine in the second place: Sincere joy; good fortune. Regrets disappear.

- Six in the third place: If you seek joy, misfortune.

- Nine in the fourth place: Haggling over joy: not yet at peace. If you avoid illness, happiness.

- Nine in the fifth place: Sincerity. In peeling, danger.

- Six at the top: Led to joy.

Image

Linked lakes: joy. This is how you should treat friends: discussing and practicing.

Joy and friendships are like linked lakes: they replenish one another. Whether fed by springs within them or by rivers flowing into them, lakes store up life-giving water in beautiful pools reflecting the light and the environment around them. Lakes offer water to all who come to drink, bathe, water their crops, or simply to cavort and be cooled on hot days of leisure. True joy is like these linked lakes: it does not stand alone, but accepts the sources of life feeding it, stores them and offers them to those drawn to the lake, and sends the waters on to a linked lake and, ultimately, to a river leading to the sea.

The qualities which nourish friendship also nurture true joys: sincerity and receptivity. However, actively or directly seeking joy is misdirected energy that tends to result in misfortune. So is haggling over joy. It is not something that can survive such dispute, though being prudent enough to avoid illness does not diminish joy but increases it.

Instead, joy is like linked lakes: based on a natural balance between receptivity and sharing. Like water, joy cannot be grasped. If it is not released and shared, it either distorts the shape of the lake by flooding or grows fetid and repulsive.

Shaughnessy, 118–119, 307–308.
Lynn, 507–511.
Wilhelm/Baynes, 223–226.

澳 (huàn) Dispersion (Spreading Waters)

Dispersion. Success. The ruler approaches the temple. Crossing the great river is effective. Persistence is effective.

- Six in the first place: For rescuing, your horse is strong. Good fortune.

- Nine in the second place: The waters reach the stairs. Regrets vanish.

- Six in the third place: The waters wash your body. No regrets.

- Six in the fourth place: The dispersion of your group. Supreme good fortune. Amid the flood there is a hill, not what your younger sister thought.

- Nine in the fifth place: Dispersion recedes at a great shout. Dispersion at the ruler's abode. No blame.

- **Nine at the top:** Dispersion of your blood. Departure with fear. No blame.

Image

When the wind moves over the watery abyss: this is the image of dispersion. Thus early rulers made offerings to the Lord on High and built temples.

When the wind blows over deep water, any objects on its surface are driven apart. Times when things fall away from each other can be frightening. Such an image of extreme fluidity seems an unlikely correlation with times when great rulers built temples and took the time to make sacrifices. Yet this hexagram equates dispersion with success and great religious and political ceremonies. It reminds us that when things seem to fall apart, this may benefit us by pushing us toward needed changes. By precluding a return to an earlier situation, dispersal forces us to persist in a new direction. At such a time we need to make sacrifices and to draw near to sources of spiritual and moral strength. Doing so is not a mark of weakness but of nobility. Even the greatest leaders have faced times when everything seemed to fall apart. They needed rituals at such times, to seek guidance and to gather their followers together. Then they could initiate great changes, ones worthy of persistence.

Shaughnessy, 160–161, 320–321.
Lynn, 511–517.
Wilhelm/Baynes, 227–230.

節 ䷂

(jié) Limitation

Limitation. Success. But bitter limitations cannot persist.

- **Nine in the first place:** Not going beyond your courtyard door: no blame.

- **Nine in the second place:** Not going beyond your courtyard gate: misfortune.

- **Six in the third place:** If you are without limits, then you will sigh and worry, but without regrets.

- **Six in the fourth place:** Contented restraint. Success.

- **Nine in the fifth place:** Sweet restraint. Good fortune. If you proceed, you will be rewarded.

- **Six at the top:** Bitter limits. Persistence brings misfortune. Regrets disappear.

Image

Above the lake, water: the image of restraint. You should set limits and act within moral guidelines.

A lake holds water within a limited space. Similarly, good people set limits to their actions, restraining themselves in order to be kind to others. The other image used here is that of the joints in bamboo, the literal meaning of the character naming this hexagram. We usually think of limits as negative, but if we think about lakes and bamboo joints, we realize that they are in fact sources of strength, essential parts of a healthy life.

Bamboo is a rapidly growing grass with hollow stems. Each hollow tube terminates in a woody membrane that blocks the hollow. These solid portions have two functions: they give strength to the plant and they are the loci for branching and other growth. Without the joints, bamboo would collapse easily, and never grow into sturdy tree-tall plants. Humans have learned to set terms to many parts of their lives. In a school or university, courses may last for a semester. This limited span makes it possible to complete one task before shifting direction or recommitting to further progress in the same field. Learning to complete short-term goals, such as a one-semester course, helps develop the skills that enable us to be more knowledgeable in selecting long-term goals and in finding methods of overcoming the obstacles that will arise within that commitment. While destructive restraints should be avoided or discarded, the appropriate limits are actually supportive. If we restrain our spending, we save enough to give ourselves more freedom of choice in the future. For this reason, Confucius taught his students to find delight in a very simple lifestyle, so that they could have the freedom to choose occupations that were not harmful to others. It is not that he loved poverty, but that he wanted his students to avoid the "golden handcuffs" or unlimited greed, and to limit economic compulsions in their lives.

Shaughnessy, 78–79, 297.
Lynn, 518–522.
Wilhelm/Baynes, 231–234.

61 中孚

(zhōng fú) Sincere to the Core

With sincerity at your core. [Even small offerings of] piglets and fish bring good fortune. Crossing the great river will work out. Persistence is effective.

- **Nine in the first place:** Calm good fortune. There are others who are not at peace.

- **Nine in the second place:** Cranes sing out from the southern bank of the river. Their young respond. I have a good wine container. I will share it with you.

- **Six in the third place:** Having acquired an enemy, sometimes advancing, sometimes resting; sometimes weeping, sometimes singing.

- **Six in the fourth place:** The moon is nearly full. The horse is missing. No blame.

- **Nine in the fifth place:** There is sincerity that unites. No blame.

- **Nine at the top**: The sound of the sacrificial bird rises to the sky. To persist will bring misfortune.

Image

On the lake, a wind—the image of sincerity at the core. You should evaluate crimes to mitigate the harshest punishments.

When wind blows across a lake, it disturbs the surface but not the depths. Similarly, the best judges, aware of truths deep in others hearts, take great care in assessing even criminal wrongs—the surface action must have a restraining response lest the community be threatened again. But unmitigated punishments cannot touch and change hearts. Fear of punishment reduces sincerity, while the goal should be an increase in this foundation of effective community.

Sincerity, or truth-telling, is of central importance in Confucianism. Without honesty, no system works well. In addition, by cultivating the ability to see and speak the truth, we make effective alliances with others possible.

Shaughnessy, 158–159, 320.
Lynn, 523–529.
Wilhelm/Baynes, 235–239.

小過 ䷽

(xiǎo guò) Minor Surplus

Minor excess. Success. Persistence is effective. You can accomplish small goals but not great deeds. A flying bird leaves a song: "Rising is inappropriate, descending apropos: great good fortune!"

- Six in the first place: A flying bird: misfortune.

- Six in the second place: Surpassing your ancestor, meeting your ancestress. You do not near your leader, but meet a helper. No blame.

- Nine in the third place: No surplus for repelling others. If you follow and attack them, misfortune.

- Nine in the fourth place: No blame. Not outdoing but meeting them. To set forth is dangerous: there must be fighting. Do not persist forever.

- Six in the fifth place: Dense clouds but no rain from our western fields. A duke shoots and takes the prey in the cave.

- **Six at the top:** Not meeting but surpassing them. The flying bird is caught in a net: misfortune. This is what is known as the calamity of inadequacy.

Image

Above the mountain, thunder: the image of a small superiority. Thus when you act, you should surpass others in respectfulness; in mourning, surpass others in sorrow; in using things, surpass others in thrift.

This hexagram describes a situation in which you have a slight advantage over those around you. The image suggests that this is similar to thunder above a mountain: not quite right, since early Chinese believed that thunder generally came from within the earth, not the sky. The older imagery here is that of a flying bird, bringing the cautionary message that it is safer not to rise too high.

The time is not yet ripe for a concerted advance, even though you may feel encouraged by some progress relative to those around you. Your strength is still only slightly superior, and thus you are too vulnerable to do much at this time. Moving ahead may seem natural, just as flying is natural to a bird. However, when hunters are near, birds are more likely to survive by remaining low to the ground, where they are camouflaged by their surroundings. If they take flight, they become visible against the sky, and attract hunters' attention with their rapid upward motion. So a time of a slight advantage is a time for restraint. Especially at such a time it is far wiser to outdo others in your respectful treatment of others, in the depth of your grief over any loss, and in your thrifty use of available resources of every kind. The situation is analogous to a time when clouds mass but have not yet produced needed rain.

In Chinese history, the situation is similar to the time when King Wu mustered his forces among his own people, before actually attacking the cruel last king of Shang. The time is one of great promise; the balance has begun to tip toward great progress. But the outcome is still in doubt. For those living under Shang at that time, little may have seemed to have changed. The king who had inherited the throne from a long line of ancestor-kings continued to reign. His army was far larger and better armed than that of Zhou, and he continued to offer royal sacrifices to the Lord on High who had sanctioned his family's rule for many generations. Wise King Wu bided his time and continued earning his reputation for honesty and keeping promises, a reputation which eventually brought decisive success to his smaller, less well-armed troops, and changed the Chinese view of the nature of real political power forever.

Shaughnessy, 92–93, 301–302.
Lynn, 530–537.
Wilhelm/Baynes, 239–244.

既濟 ䷾

(jì jì) After the Crossing

After the crossing. Success. In what is minor, persistence pays. In the beginning, good fortune. In the end, disorder.

- **Nine in the first place:** Dragging your ribbon, wetting your tail. No blame.

- **Six in the second place:** The woman loses her hair ornament. Do not pursue it, for in seven days you will obtain one.

- **Nine in the third place:** The lofty Ancestors attacked the demon country, and conquered it in three years. Do not deal with petty people.

- **Six in the fourth place:** The jacket is padded with silk wadding. All day, take warning.

- **Nine in the fifth place:** Though your neighbor to the east slaughters an ox for his sacrifice, it is not as effective as the offering of wild herbage by your neighbor to the west, which really provides prosperity. Good fortune.

- **Six at the top:** Wetting your head: danger.

Image

Water above the fire: the image of having completed a crossing. You should think about calamities and make preparations to prevent them.

This—the most fruitful of conditions, when one has completed the ferry ride across the hazardous stream—is likened to placing water over the fire, a position in which cooking may be accomplished, or flames doused, if need be. Yet even in this time of great relief at having escaped a series of obvious threats and safely reached your destination, the *Changes* reminds you that though you see no dangers now, some are inevitable in the future. For this reason, while we may enjoy our successes, it is provident to use such times to prepare for future dangers. It is never safe to rest on our laurels. Instead, we must use times of reduced stress and relative prosperity to set aside savings for unforeseen emergencies, since these are inevitable components in every person's life, no matter how apparently secure.

Having found a place where it is safe to rebuild, do so with care and caution. In escaping from great dangers, we develop skills in sensing and responding to danger, and these skills will remain useful even after dangers are past. We must analyze the possibilities of our current conditions and learn from previous mistakes. A certain level of thoughtful awareness of life's normal threats is not useless anxiety but a way of avoiding later troubles. Thus, we balance our relief and joy with care in preventing future ills.

Shaughnessy, 80–81, 298.
Lynn, 538–544.
Wilhelm/Baynes, 244–248.

未濟 ䷿

(wèi jì) Not Yet Across

Not yet across. Success. The young fox, nearly having completed his fording of the river, gets its tail wet. No destination works out.

- Six in the first place: Getting its tail wet. Distress.

- Nine in the second place: Dragging its sash. Persistence brings good fortune.

- Six in the third place: Not yet across the ford. To campaign brings misfortune. It is beneficial to ford the great river.

- Nine in the fourth place: Persistence brings good fortune. Remorse disappears. Thundering, using arms against the "demon-land." After three years, there will be the reward of a great nation.

- Six in the fifth place: Persistence brings good fortune, without regrets. The radiance of the best kind of person: having sincerity. Good fortune.

- **Nine at the top:** Having sincerity with drinking of wine, without troubles. Dipping its head, there is sincerity.

Image

Fire above the water: the image of not completing the ford of the stream. You should make distinctions carefully, and place others appropriately.

Flames above water represent a transition halted before it is complete. The hexagram describes a fox kit scampering across a frozen river. But just before he reaches safety on the other side, he lets his tail droop. If it freezes to the ice, it traps the fox in an extremely dangerous position in the open, vulnerable to predators.

This image reminds us of the dangers which may arise when success seems within our grasp. Our final steps to safety need to be taken with as much caution as the first.

Shaughnessy, 144–145, 316.
Lynn, 545–551.
Wilhelm/Baynes, 248–252.

The Zhou Text

The received text with select revisions based
on Mawangdui text (from Shaughnessy [1996])

1 ䷀ 乾 The Creative

乾元亨利貞。

初九　潛龍勿用。

九二　見龍在田。利見大人。

九三　君子終日乾乾。

　　　夕惕若厲。无咎。

九四　或躍在淵。无咎。

九五　飛龍在天。利見大人。

上九　亢龍有悔。

用九　見羣龍无首。吉。

　　　~象~

天行健，君子以自強不息。

2 ䷁ 坤 Earth, The Receptive

坤元亨利牝馬之貞。

君子有攸往。先迷後得。主利。

西南得朋。

東北喪朋。安貞吉。

初六　履霜堅冰至。

六二　直方大。不習无不利。

六三　含章可貞。或從王事。

　　　无成有終。

六四　括囊。无咎无譽。

六五　黃裳。元吉。

上六　龍戰于野。其血玄黃。

用六　利永貞。

　　　~象~

地勢坤，君子以厚德載物。

3 ䷂ 坤 Sprouting

坤元亨利貞。勿用有攸往。

利建侯。

初九　磐桓。利居貞。利建侯。

六二　屯如邅如。乘馬班如。

　　　匪寇婚媾。女子貞不字。

　　　十年乃字。

六三　即鹿無虞。惟入于林

　　　中。君子幾不如舍。往吝。

六四　乘馬班如。求婚媾。

　　　往吉。无不利。

九五　屯其膏。小貞吉。

　　　大貞凶。

上六　乘馬班如。泣血漣如。

　　　~象~

雲，雷，屯；君子以經綸。

4 ䷃ 蒙 New Grass

蒙亨。匪我求童蒙。童蒙求我。

初筮告。再三瀆。瀆則不告。

利貞。

初六　發蒙。利用刑人。

　　　用說桎梏。以往吝。

九二　包蒙吉。納婦吉。

　　　子克家。

六三　勿用取女。見金夫。

　　　不有躬。无攸利。

六四　困蒙。吝。

六五　童蒙。吉。

上九　擊蒙。不利為寇。

　　　利禦寇。

　　　~象~

山下出泉，蒙；君子以果行育德。

5 ䷄ 需 Waiting

需有孚。光亨貞吉。利涉大川。

初九 需于郊。利用恆。无咎。

九二 需于沙。小有言。終吉。

九三 需于泥。致寇至。

六四 需于血。出自穴。

九五 需于酒食。貞吉。

上六 入于穴。有不速之客三
人來。敬之終吉。

~象~

雲上於天，需；
君子以飲食宴樂。

6 ䷅ 訟 Strife

訟有孚。窒惕。中吉。終凶。
利見大人。不利涉大川。

初六 不永所事。小有言。
終吉。

九二 不克訟。歸而逋其邑。
人三百戶。无眚。

六三 食舊德。貞。厲終吉。
或從王事。无成。

九四 不克訟。復即命。
渝安貞。吉。

九五 訟。元吉。

上九 或錫之鞶帶。
終朝三褫之。

~象~

天與水違行，訟；
君子以作事謀始。

7 ䷆ 師

With a Multitude of Followers

師貞。丈人吉。无咎。

初六 師出以律。否臧凶。

九二 在師中吉。无咎。
王三錫命。

六三 師或輿尸。凶。

六四 師左次。无咎。

六五 田有禽。利執言。
无咎。長子帥師。
弟子輿尸。貞凶。

上六 大君有命。開國承家。
小人勿用。

~象~

地中有水，師；
君子以容民畜眾。

8 ䷇ 比 Closeness with Others

比吉。原筮元永貞。无咎。
不寧方來。後夫凶。

初六 有孚比之。无咎。
有孚盈缶。終來有它吉。

六二 比之自內。貞吉。

六三 比之匪人。

六四 外比之。貞吉。

九五 顯比。王用三驅。
失前禽。邑人不誡。吉。

上六 比之无首。凶。

~象~

地上有水，比；先王以建萬國，
親諸侯。

9 ䷈ 小畜 The Smaller Herd

小畜亨。密雲不雨。自我西茭。

初九　復自道。何其咎。吉。

九二　牽復。吉。

九三　輿說輻。夫妻反目。

六四　有孚。血去惕出。
　　　无咎。

九五　有孚攣如。富以其鄰。

上九　既雨既處。尚德載。
　　　婦貞厲。月幾望。
　　　君子征凶。

~象~

風行天上，小畜：
君子以懿文德。

10 ䷉ 履 Stepping

履虎尾。不咥人。亨。

初九　素履往。无咎。

九二　履道坦坦。幽人貞吉。

六三　眇能視。跛能履。
　　　履虎尾。咥人凶。
　　　武人為于大君。

九四　履虎尾。愬愬終吉。

九五　夬履。貞厲。

上九　視履考祥。其旋元吉。

~象~

上天下澤，履；君子以辨上下，
安民志。

11 ䷊ 泰 Peace

泰小往大來。吉亨。

初九　拔茅茹。以其彙。
　　　征吉。

九二　包荒。用馮河。不遐
　　　遺。朋亡。得尚于中行。

九三　无平不陂。无往不復。
　　　艱貞无咎。勿恤其孚。
　　　于食有福。

六四　翩翩。不富以其鄰。
　　　不戒以孚。

六五　帝乙歸妹。以祉元吉。

上六　城復于隍。勿用師。
　　　自邑告命。貞吝。

~象~

天地交泰，后以財(裁)成天地之
道，輔相天地之宜，以左右民。

12 ䷋ 否 Obstruction (Stagnation)

否之匪人。不利君子貞。
大往小來。

初六　拔茅茹。以其彙。
　　　貞吉。亨。

六二　包承。小人吉。
　　　大人否。亨。

六三　包羞。

九四　有命无咎。疇離祉。

九五　休否。大人吉。
　　　其亡其亡。繫于苞桑。

上九　傾否。先否後喜。

~象~

天地不交，否；
君子以儉德辟難，不可榮以祿。

13 ䷌ 同人 Friendship

同人于野。亨。利涉大川。
利君子貞。

初九　同人于門。无咎。
六二　同人于宗。吝。
九三　伏戎于莽。升其高陵。
　　　三歲不興。
九四　乘其墉。弗克攻。吉。
九五　同人先號咷而後笑。
　　　大師克相遇。
上九　同人于郊。无悔。

~象~

天與火，同人；
君子以類族辨物。

14 ䷍ 大有 Great Possession

大有元亨。

初九　无交害。匪咎。
　　　艱則无咎。
九二　大車以載。有攸往。
　　　无咎。
九三　公用亨于天子。
　　　小人弗克。
九四　匪其彭。无咎。
六五　厥孚交如。威如。吉。
上九　自天祐之。吉无不利。

~象~

火在天上，大有；
君子以竭惡揚善，順天休命。

15 ䷎ 謙 Modesty

謙亨。君子有終。

初六　謙謙君子。用涉大川。
　　　吉。
六二　鳴謙。貞吉。
九三　勞謙君子。有終吉。
六四　无不利撝謙。
六五　不富以其鄰。
　　　利用侵伐。无不利。

上六　鳴謙。利用行師。
　　　征邑國。

~象~

地中有山，謙；
君子以裒多益寡，稱物平施。

16 ䷏ 餘 Excess

餘利建侯行師。

初六　鳴餘。凶。
六二　疥于石。不終日。
　　　貞吉。
六三　杆餘悔。遲有悔。
九四　允餘。大有得。勿疑。
　　　朋甲譖。
九四　允餘。大有得。勿疑。
　　　朋甲讒。
六五　貞疾。恆不死。
上六　冥餘。成有諭。无咎。

~象~

雷出地奮，餘。
先王以作樂崇德，殷荐之上帝，
以配祖考。

17 ䷐ 隨 Following

隨元亨利貞。无咎。

　　初九 官有渝。貞吉。

　　　　出門交有功。

　　六二 係小子。失丈夫。

　　六三 係丈夫。失小子。

　　　　隨有求得。利居貞。

　　九四 隨有獲。貞凶。

　　　　有復在道以盟。何咎。

　　九五 復于嘉。吉。

　　上六 拘係之。乃從維之。

　　　　王用芳于西山。

　　　　～象～

澤中有雷，隨;

君子以嚮晦入宴息。

18 ䷑ 箇 Branching Out

箇元亨。利涉大川。先甲三日。
後甲三日。

　　初六 榦父之箇。有子。

　　　　巧无咎。厲終吉。

　　九二 榦母之箇。不可貞。

　　九三 榦父之箇。小有悔。

　　　　无大咎。

　　六四 浴父之箇。往見吝。

　　六五 榦父之箇。用輿。

　　上九 不事王侯。高尚其德兌。

　　　　～象～

山下有風，箇;

君子以振民育德。

19 ䷒ 林 The Forest

林元亨利貞。至于八月有凶。

　　初九 禁林貞吉。

　　九二 禁林吉。无不利。

　　六三 甘林。无攸利。

　　　　既憂之。无咎。

　　六四 至林。无咎。

　　六五 知林。大君之宜。吉。

　　上六 敦林。吉。无咎。

　　　　～象～

澤上有地，林;

君子以教思無窮，容保民無疆。

20 ䷓ 觀 Gazing (Contemplation)

觀盥而不薦。有孚顒若。

　　初六 童觀。小人无咎。

　　　　君子吝。

　　六二 闚觀。利女貞。

　　六三 觀我生進退。

　　六四 觀國之光。

　　　　利用賓于王。

　　九五 觀我生。君子无咎。

　　上九 觀其生。君子无咎。

　　　　～象～

風行地上，觀; 先王以省方，
觀民設教。

21 ䷔ 噬嗑 Taking a Bite

噬嗑亨。利用獄。

初九 履校滅趾。无咎。

六二 噬膚滅鼻。无咎。

六三 噬腊肉。遇毒。少吝。
　　 无咎。

九四 噬乾胏。得毒矢。
　　 利艱貞。吉。

六五 噬乾肉。得毒。貞厲。
　　 无咎。

上九 荷校滅耳。凶。

~象~

雷電噬嗑；先王以明罰敕法。

22 ䷕ 賁 Elegance

賁亨。小利有攸往。

初九 賁其趾。舍車而徒。

六二 賁其須。

九三 賁如濡如。永貞吉。

六四 賁如皤如。白馬翰如。
　　 匪寇婚媾。

六五 賁于丘園。束帛戔戔。
　　 吝。終吉。

上九 白賁。无咎。

~象~

山下有火，賁；君子以明庶政，
無敢折獄。

23 ䷖ 剝 Peeling

剝不利有攸往。

初六 剝牀以足。蔑貞凶。

六二 剝牀以辨。蔑貞凶。

六三 剝之无咎。

六四 剝牀以膚。凶。

六五 貫魚。食宮人寵。
　　 无不利。

上九 碩果不食。君子得車。
　　 小人剝廬。

~象~

山附地上，剝；
上以厚下，安宅。

24 ䷗ 復 Returning

復亨。出入无疾。堋來无咎。

反復其道。七日來復。

利有攸往。

初九 不遠復。无祗悔。
　　 元吉。

六二 休復。吉。

六三 頻復。厲。无咎。

六四 中行獨復。

六五 敦復。无悔。

上六 迷復。凶。有災眚。
　　 用行師。終有大敗。
　　 以其國君凶。
　　 至于十年不克征。

~象~

雷在地中，復；
先王以至日閉關，商旅不行，
后不省方。

25 ䷘ 无妄 Not False

无妄元亨利貞。其匪正有眚。
不利有攸往。

初九 无妄。往吉。

六二 不耕穫。不菑畬。
則利有攸往。

六三 无妄之災。或繫之牛。
行人之得。邑人之災。

九四 可貞。无咎。

九五 无妄之疾。勿藥有喜。

上九 无妄。行有眚。
无攸利。

~象~

天下雷行，物與無妄；
先王以茂對時，育萬物。

26 ䷙ 大畜 Great Nurturing

大畜利貞。不家食。吉。
利涉大川。

初九 有厲。利已。

九二 輿說輹。

九三 良馬逐。利艱貞。
曰閑輿衛。利有攸往。

六四 童牛之牿。元吉。

六五 豶豕之牙。吉。

上九 何天之衢。亨。

~象~

天在山中，大畜；
君子以多識前言往行，
以畜其德。

27 ䷚ 頤 Jaws

頤貞吉。觀頤。自求口實。

初九 舍爾靈龜。觀我朵頤。
凶。

六二 顛頤。拂經于北。
頤征凶。

六三 拂頤。貞凶。
十年勿用。无攸利。

六四 顛頤。吉。虎視眈眈。
其欲逐逐。无咎。

六五 拂經。居貞吉。
不可涉大川。

上九 由頤。厲吉。利涉大川。

~象~

山下有雷，頤；君子以慎言語，
節飲食。

28 ䷛ 大過 Greatly Surpassing

大過棟橈。利有攸往。亨。

初六 藉用白茅。无咎。

九二 枯楊生稊。
老夫得其女妻。无不利。

九三 棟橈。凶。

九四 棟橈。吉。有它吝。

九五 枯楊生華。
老婦得其士夫。无咎无譽。

上六 過涉滅頂。凶。无咎。

~象~

澤滅木，大過；
君子以獨立不懼，遯世無悶。

29 ䷜ 坎 The Abyss

坎有孚。維心亨。行有尚。

初六 習坎。入于坎窞。凶。

九二 坎有險。求小得。

六三 來之坎坎。險且枕。

入于坎窞。勿用。

六四 樽酒簋貳。用缶。

納約自牖。終无咎。

九五 坎不盈。祗既平。

无咎。

上六 係用徽纆。寘于叢棘。

三歲不得。凶。

~象~

水 至，習坎；君子以常德行，
習教事。

30 ䷝ 羅 The Net

羅利貞。亨。畜牝牛。吉。

初九 履昔然。敬之。无咎。

六二 黃羅。元吉。

九三 日昃之羅。不鼓缶而歌。

則大耋之嗟。凶。

九四 出如其來如。焚如。

死如。棄如。

六五 出涕沱若。戚嗟若。吉。

上九 王用出征。有嘉。

折首。獲匪其醜。无咎。

~象~

明兩作離，
大人以繼明照于四方。

31 ䷞ 咸 Reciprocity, Respect

咸亨。利貞。取女吉。

初六 咸其拇。

六二 咸其腓。凶。居吉。

九三 咸其股。執其隨。

往吝。

九四 貞吉悔亡。憧憧往來。

朋從爾思。

九五 咸其脢。无悔。

上六 咸其輔頰舌。

~象~

山上有澤，咸；君子以虛受人。

32 ䷟ 恆 Duration

恆亨。无咎。利貞。利有攸往。

初六 浚恆貞凶。无攸利。

九二 悔亡。

九三 不恆其德。或承之羞。

貞吝。

九四 田无禽。

六五 恒其德貞。婦人吉。

夫子凶。

上六 振恆凶。

~象~

雷風，恆；君子以立不易方。

33 ䷠ 遯 Retreat

遯亨。小利貞。

初六　遯尾厲。勿用有攸往。

六二　執之用黃牛之革。
　　　莫之勝說。

九三　係遯。有疾厲。
　　　畜臣妾吉。

九四　好遯。君子吉。
　　　小人否。

九五　嘉遯貞吉。

上九　肥遯无不利。

~象~

天下有山，遯；君子以遠小人，
不惡而嚴。

34 ䷡ 大壯 Great Strength

大壯利貞。

初九　壯于趾。征凶有復。

九二　貞吉。

九三　小人用壯。君子用罔。
　　　貞厲。羝羊觸藩。羸其角。

九四　貞吉。悔亡。藩決不
　　　羸。壯于大輿之輹。

六五　喪羊于易。无悔。

上六　羝羊觸藩。不能退。
　　　不能遂。无攸利。艱則吉。

~象~

雷在天上，大壯；
君子以非禮勿履。

35 ䷢ 晉 Advancing

晉康侯用錫馬蕃庶。晝日三接。

初六　晉如摧如。貞吉。罔
　　　孚。裕无咎。

六二　晉如愁如。貞吉。
　　　受茲介福。于其王母。

六三　眾允悔亡。

九四　晉如鼫鼠。貞厲。

六五　悔亡。失得勿恤。
　　　往吉无不利。

上九　晉其角。維用伐邑。
　　　厲吉无咎。貞吝。

~象~

明出地上，晉；
君子以自昭明德。

36 ䷣ 明夷 Wounded Light

明夷利艱貞。

初九　明夷于飛。垂其左翼。
　　　君子于行。三日不食。
　　　有攸往。主人有言。

六二　明夷。夷于左股。
　　　用拯馬壯吉。

九三　明夷于南狩。得其大
　　　首。不可疾貞。

六四　入于左腹。獲明夷之
　　　心。于出門庭。

六五　箕子之明夷。利貞。

上六　不明晦。初登于天。
　　　後入于地。

~象~

明入地中，明夷；君子以蒞眾，
用晦而明。

37 ䷤ 家人 Family

家人利女貞。

初九 門有家。悔亡。

六二 无攸遂。在中饋。
　　　貞吉。

九三 家人嗃嗃。悔厲吉。
　　　婦子嘻嘻。終吝。

六四 富家大吉。

九五 王假有家。勿恤吉。

上九 有孚威如。終吉。

~象~

風自火出，家人；

君子以言有物，而行有恆。

38 ䷥ 睽 Double Vision

睽小事吉。

初九 悔亡。喪馬勿逐自復。
　　　見惡人。无咎。

九二 遇主于巷。无咎。

六三 見輿曳。其牛掣。
　　　其人天且劓。无初有終。

九四 睽孤。遇元夫。交孚。
　　　厲无咎。

六五 悔亡。登宗噬膚。
　　　往何咎。

上九 睽孤。見豕負塗。
　　　載鬼一車。先張之弧。
　　　後說之弧。匪寇婚媾。
　　　往遇雨則吉。

~象~

上火下澤，睽；君子以同而異。

39 ䷦ 蹇 Impeded

蹇利西南。不利東北。

利見大人。貞吉。

初六 往蹇來譽。

六二 王臣蹇蹇。匪躬之故。

九三 往蹇來反。

六四 往蹇來連。

九五 大蹇朋來。

上六 往蹇來碩。吉。
　　　利見大人。

~象~

山上有水，蹇；

君子以反身修德。

40 ䷧ 解 Released (Untied)

解利西南。无所往。其來復吉。

有攸往。夙吉。

初六 无咎。

九二 田獲三狐。得黃矢。
　　　貞吉。

六三 負且乘。致寇至。貞吝。

九四 解其拇。朋至此復。

六五 君子維有解。吉。
　　　有復于小人。

上六 公用射隼于高墉之上。
　　　獲之无不利。

~象~

雷雨作，解；君子以赦過宥罪。

41 ䷨ 損 Decrease

損有孚。元吉。无咎可貞。
利有攸往。曷之用。二簋可用享。

初九 已事遄往。无咎。
　　酌損之。
九二 利貞。征凶。弗損益
　　之。
六三 三人行。則損一人。
　　一人行。則得其友。
六四 損其疾。使遄有喜。
　　无咎。
六五 或益之十朋之龜。
　　弗克回。元吉。
上九 弗損益之。无咎。
　　貞吉。利有攸往。
　　得臣无家。

~象~

山下有澤，損；君子以懲忿窒欲。

42 ䷩ 益 Increase

益利有攸往。利涉大川。

初九 利用為大作。元吉无咎。
六二 或益之十朋之龜。
　　弗克回。永貞吉。
　　王用享于帝吉。
六三 益之用凶事。无咎。
　　有孚中行。告公用圭。
六四 中行。告公從。
　　利用為依遷國。
九五 有孚惠心。勿問元吉。
　　有孚惠我德。
上九 莫益之。或擊之。
　　立心勿恆。凶。

~象~

風雷，益；君子以見善則遷，
有過則改。

43 ䷪ 夬 Resolute Action

夬揚于王庭。孚號有厲。
告自邑。不利即戎。利有攸往。

初九 壯于前趾。往不勝為咎。
九二 惕號。莫夜有戎。勿恤。
九三 壯于頄。有凶。
　　君子夬夬。獨行遇雨。
　　若濡有慍。无咎。
九四 臀无膚。其行次且。
　　牽羊悔亡。聞言不信。
九五 莧陸夬夬。中行无咎。
上六 无號。終有凶。

~象~

澤上于天，夬；
君子以施祿及下，居德則忌。

44 ䷫ 姤 The Royal Bride

姤女壯。勿用取女。

初六 繫于金柅。貞吉。有攸
　　往。見凶。贏豕孚蹢躅。
九二 包有魚。无咎。不利賓。
九三 臀无膚。其行次且。
　　厲。无大咎。
九四 包无魚。正凶。
九五 以杞包瓜。含章。
　　有隕自天。
上九 姤其角。吝。无咎。

~象~

天下有風，姤；后以施命誥四方。

45 ䷬ 萃 Gathered Together

萃亨。王假有廟。利見大人。
亨。利貞。用大牲吉。
利有攸往。

初六　有孚不終。乃亂乃萃。
　　　若號一握為笑。勿恤。
　　　往无咎。
六二　引吉无咎。
　　　孚乃利用禴。
六三　萃如嗟如。无攸利。
　　　往无咎。小吝。
九四　大吉无咎。
九五　萃有位。无咎匪孚。
　　　元永貞。悔亡。
上六　齎咨涕洟。无咎。

~象~

澤上於地，萃；君子以除戎器，
戒不虞。

46 ䷭ 升 Pushing Upwards

升元亨。用見大人。勿恤。
南征吉。

初六　允升大吉。
九二　孚乃利用禴。无咎。
九三　升虛邑。
六四　王用亨于岐山。吉。
　　　无咎。
六五　貞吉升階。
上六　冥升。利于不息之貞。

~象~

地中生木，升；君子以順德，
積小以高大。

47 ䷮ 困 Exhaustion

困亨。貞大人吉。无咎。
有言不信。

初六　臀困于株木。
　　　入于幽谷。三歲不覿。
九二　困于酒食。朱紱方來。
　　　利用享祀。征凶无咎。
六三　困于石。據于蒺藜。
　　　入于其宮。不見其妻。凶。
九四　來徐徐。困于金車。
　　　吝。有終。
九五　劓刖。困于赤紱。
　　　乃徐有說。利用祭祀。
上六　困于葛藟。于臲卼。
　　　曰動悔有悔。貞吉。

~象~

澤無水，困；君子以致命遂志。

48 ䷯ 井 The Well

井改邑不改井。无喪无得。
往來井井。汔至亦未繘井。
羸其瓶。凶。

初六　井泥不食。舊井无禽。
九二　井谷射鮒。甕敝漏。
九三　井渫不食。為我心惻。
　　　可用汲。王明。
　　　並受其福。
六四　井甃无咎。
九五　井冽。寒泉食。
上六　井收勿幕。有孚元吉。

~象~

木上有水，井；
君子以勞民勸相。

49 ䷰ 革 Molting (Shedding)

革已日乃復。元亨。利貞。
悔亡。

初九　鞏用黃牛之革。

六二　已日乃革之。
　　　征吉无咎。

九三　征凶貞厲。革言三就。
　　　有復。

九四　悔亡有孚。改命吉。

九五　大人虎變。未占有復。

上六　君子豹變。小人革面。
　　　征凶。居貞吉。

~象~

澤中有火，革；
君子以治歷明時。

50 ䷱ 鼎 The Cauldron

鼎元吉。亨。

初六　鼎顛趾。利出否。
　　　得妾以其子。无咎。

九二　鼎有實。我仇有疾。
　　　不我能即。吉。

九三　鼎耳革。其行塞。
　　　雉膏不食。方雨虧悔。
　　　終吉。

九四　鼎折足。覆公餗。
　　　其刑渥。凶。

六五　鼎黃耳金鉉。利貞。

上九　鼎玉鉉。大吉。
　　　无不利。

~象~

木上有火，鼎；
君子以正位凝命。

51 ䷲ 震 Thunder

震亨。震來虩虩。笑言啞啞。
震驚百里。不喪匕鬯。

初九　震來虩虩。
　　　後笑言啞啞。吉。

六二　震來厲。億喪貝。
　　　躋于九陵。勿逐。七日得。

六三　震蘇蘇。震行无眚。

九四　震遂泥。

六五　震往來厲。
　　　意无喪有事。

上六　震索索。視矍矍。
　　　征凶。震不于其躬。
　　　于其鄰。
　　　无咎。婚媾有言。

~象~

洊雷，震；君子以恐懼修身。

52 ䷳ 艮 Stillness

艮其背。不獲其身。行其庭。
不見其人。无咎。

初六　艮其止。无咎。
　　　利永貞。

六二　艮其腓。不拯其隨。
　　　其心不快。

九三　艮其限。列其夤。
　　　厲熏心。

六四　艮其身。无咎。

六五　艮其輔。言有序。
　　　悔亡。

上九　敦艮吉。

~象~

兼山，艮；君子以思不出其位。

53 ䷴ 漸 Gradual Progress

漸女歸吉。利貞。

初六　鴻漸于淵。
　　　小子厲有言。無咎。

六二　鴻漸于坂。酒食衎衎。
　　　吉。

九三　鴻漸于陸。夫征不復。
　　　婦孕不育。凶。利禦寇。

六四　鴻漸于木。或得其桷。
　　　无咎。

九五　鴻漸于陵。婦三歲不孕。
　　　終莫之勝。吉。

上九　鴻漸于陸。
　　　其羽可用為儀。吉。

~象~

山上有木，漸；君子以居賢德，
善俗。

54 ䷵ 歸妹 Coming Home

歸妹征凶。无攸利。

初九　歸妹以娣。跛能履。
　　　征吉。

九二　眇能視。利幽人之貞。

六三　歸妹以須。反歸以娣。

九四　歸妹愆期。遲歸有時。

六五　帝乙歸妹。其君之袂。
　　　不如其娣之袂良。
　　　月幾望吉。

上六　女承筐无實。
　　　士刲羊无血。无攸利。

~象~

澤上有雷，歸妹；
君子以永終知敝。

55 ䷶ 豐 Abundance

豐亨。王假之。勿憂。宜日中。

初九　遇其配主。雖旬无咎。
　　　往有尚。

六二　豐其蔀。日中見斗。
　　　往得疑疾。有復發若。吉。

九三　豐其沛。日中見沬。
　　　折其右肱。无咎。

九四　豐其蔀。日中見斗。
　　　遇其夷主。吉。

六五　來章。有慶譽吉。

上六　豐其屋。蔀其家。
　　　闚其戶。闃其无人。
　　　三歲不覿。凶。

~象~

雷電皆至，豐；君子以折獄致刑。

56 ䷷ 旅 The Wanderer

旅小亨。旅貞吉。

初六　旅瑣瑣。斯其所取火。

六二　旅即次。懷其茨。
　　　得童僕貞。

九三　旅焚其次。喪其童僕。
　　　貞厲。

九四　旅于處。得其資斧。
　　　我心不快。

六五　射雉。一矢亡。
　　　終以譽命。

上九　鳥焚其巢。旅人先笑後
　　　號咷。喪牛于易。凶。

~象~

山上有火，旅；
君子以明慎用刑，而不留獄。

57 ☴ 巽 Calculation, Choosing

巽小亨。利有攸往。利見大人。

　初六　進退。利武人之貞。
　九二　巽在牀下。用史巫
　　　　紛若。吉。无咎。
　九三　頻巽吝。
　六四　悔亡。田獲三品。
　九五　貞吉悔亡。无不利。
　　　　无初有終。先庚三日。
　　　　後庚三日。吉。
　上九　巽在牀下。喪其資斧。
　　　　貞凶。

~象~

隨風，巽；君子以申命行事。

58 ☱ 兌 Joy

兌亨。小利貞。

　初九　和兌吉。
　九二　孚兌吉。悔亡。
　六三　來兌凶。
　九四　商兌未寧。介疾有喜。
　九五　孚于剝。有厲。
　上六　引兌。

~象~

麗澤，兌；君子以朋友講習。

59 ☴ 渙 Dispersion (Spreading Waters)

渙亨。王假有廟。利涉大川。
利貞。

　初六　用拯馬壯吉。悔亡。
　九二　渙奔其阶。悔亡。
　六三　渙其躬。无悔。
　六四　渙其羣元吉。渙有丘。
　　　　匪娣所思。
　九五　渙汗其人號。渙。
　　　　王居无咎。
　上九　渙其血。去逖出。
　　　　无咎。

~象~

風行水上，渙；
先王以享于帝立廟。

60 ☵ 節 Limitation

節亨。苦節不可貞。

　初九　不出戶庭。无咎。
　九二　不出門庭。凶。
　六三　不節若。則嗟若。
　　　　无咎。
　六四　安節亨。
　九五　甘節吉。往有尚。
　上六　苦節貞凶。悔亡。

~象~

澤上有水，節；君子以制數度，
議德行。

61 ䷼ 中孚 Sincere to the Core

中孚豚魚吉。利涉大川。利貞。

初九 虞吉。有他不燕。

九二 鳴鶴在陰。其子和之。
我有好爵。吾與爾靡之。

六三 得敵。或鼓或罷。
或泣或歌。

六四 月幾望。馬匹亡。无咎。

九五 有孚攣如。无咎。

上九 翰音登于天。貞凶。

~象~

澤上有風，中孚；
君子以議獄緩死。

62 ䷽ 小過 Minor Surplus

小過亨。利貞。可小事。
不可大事。飛鳥遺之音。
不宜上宜下。大吉。

初六 飛鳥以凶。

六二 過其祖。遇其妣。不及
其君。遇其臣。无咎。

九三 弗過防之。從或戕之。
凶。

九四 无咎。弗過遇之。
往厲必戒。勿用永貞。

六五 密雲不雨。自我西郊。
公弋取彼在穴。

上六 弗遇過之。飛鳥羅之。
凶。是謂災眚。

~象~

山上有雷，小過；
君子以行過乎恭，喪過乎哀，
用過乎儉。

63 ䷾ 既濟 After the Crossing

既濟亨小。利貞。初吉。終亂。

初九 曳其綸。濡其尾。
无咎。

六二 婦喪其茀。勿逐。
七日得。

九三 高宗伐鬼方。
三年克之。小人勿用。

六四 繻有衣袽。終日戒。

九五 東鄰殺牛。不如西鄰之
禴祭。實受其福。

上六 濡其首。厲。

~象~

水在火上，既濟；
君子以思患而預防之。

64 ䷿ 未濟 Not Yet Across

未濟亨。小狐汔濟。濡其尾。
无攸利。

初六 濡其尾。吝。

九二 抴其綸。貞吉。

六三 未濟征凶。利涉大川。

九四 貞吉悔亡。
震用伐鬼方。
三年有賞于大國。

六五 貞吉无悔。君子之光。
有孚吉。

上九 有孚于飲酒。无咎。
濡其首。有孚。

~象~

火在水上，未濟；
君子以慎辨物居方。

Further Reading

One of the best ways to seek the meaning behind the words of translations is to compare several good ones. This can be particularly useful for texts as difficult to interpret as the *Book of Changes* and the *Laozi*, where there are several valid interpretations for laconic and difficult texts. For this reason, I encourage readers to consult these helpful works.

• Other efforts to discern the earliest meanings, stripped of commentaries:

Richard A. Kunst, "The Original Yijing: A Text, Phonetic Transcription, Translation and Indexes, with Sample Glosses" Ph.D. dissertation (Berkeley: University of California, Berkeley, 1985).

Richard Rutt, *Zhouyi: the Book of Changes, a Bronze Age Document Translated with Introduction and Notes* (London: Routledge Curzon, 1996 and 2002).

Edward Shaughnessy, *I Ching: The Classic of Changes, the First English Translation of the Newly Discovered Second-century B.C. Mawangdui Texts* (New York: Ballantine Books, 1996).

- Translations and analysis based on post-Han commentaries:

Richard John Lynn, *The Classic of Changes: A New Translation of the I Ching as Interpreted by Wang Bi* (New York: Columbia University Press, 1994).

Richard Wilhelm and Cary F. Baynes, *The I Ching or Book of Changes* (Princeton: Princeton University Press, 1950, 1967).

- I have also recommended readings as the next steps in a variety of directions supporting a deeper understanding. In doing so, I have not tried to be exhaustive but to lead the reader towards sources that provide gateways to the many riches of Chinese history and thought.

Patricia Ebrey, *Cambridge Illustrated History of China* (Cambridge: Cambridge University Press). First two chapters.

David Keightley, "Oracle Bone Inscriptions of the Late Shang Dynasty," in *Sources of Chinese Tradition, volume I,* second edition. Edited by William Theodore DeBary, Irene Bloom, et al. (New York: Columbia University Press, 1999). Pages 3–23.

- For more examples of some types of early Chinese reasoning, from natural/human juxtapositions, experiential data, and reasoning based on both:

The Book of Songs (Shijing): The Ancient Chinese Classic of Poetry, translated from the Chinese by Arthur Waley, edited with additional translations by Joseph R. Allen (New York: Grove Press, 1996).

The Tso Chuan: Selections from China's Oldest Narrative History, translated by Burton Watson (New York: Columbia University Press, 1989).

Xunzi: Basic Writings, translated by Burton Watson (New York: Columbia University Press, 2003).

• Recent secondary sources include:

The Cambridge History of Ancient China, edited by Michael Loewe and Edward Shaughnessy (Cambridge: Cambridge University Press, 1999).

Defining Chu: Image and Reality in Ancient China, edited by Constance A. Cook and John S. Major, (Honolulu, University of Hawai'i Press, 1999).

Michael Nylan, *The Five "Confucian" Classics* (New Haven: Yale University Press, 2001).

Yuri Pines, *Foundations of Confucian Thought: Intellectual Life During the Chunqiu Period, 722-453 B.C.E.* (Honolulu: University of Hawai'i Press, 2002).

• On feminist and *yin/yang* issues:

Alison Harley Black, "Gender and Cosmology in Chinese Correlative Thinking," in *Gender and Religion: On the Complexity of Symbols,* edited by Carolyn Walker Bynum, Stevan Harrel, and Paula Richman (Boston: Beacon Press, 1986).

Lisa Ann Raphals, *Sharing the Light: Representations of Women and Virtue in Early China* (Albany: State University of New York Press, 1998).

Vitaly Rubin, "The Concepts of Wu-hsing and Yin-yang," in *Journal of Chinese Philosophy* 9 (1982). Pages 131–157.

- On divination:

Ssu-ma Ch'ien (Sima Qian), "Biographies of the Diviners of Lucky Days," in *Records of the Grand Historian of China,* translated by Burton Watson (New York: Columbia University Press, 1961, 1968), vol. II. Pages 468–475.

Donald Harper, "Warring States Natural Philosophy and Occult Thought," in *The Cambridge History of Ancient China,* edited by Michael Loewe and Edward Shaughnessy (Cambridge: Cambridge University Press, 1999). Pages 813–884.

Kidder Smith, "The I Ching Prior to Sung," in *Sung Dynasty Uses of the I Ching,* edited by Kidder Smith, Peter K. Bol, Joseph A. Allen, and Don J. Wyatt (Princeton: Princeton University Press, 1990).

For more recommended reading, presentations and videos visit originaliching.org.

Bibliography

Book of Songs, tr. Bernhard Karlgren (Stockholm: Museum of Far Eastern Antiquities, 1950).

Chung-ying Cheng, "Inquiring into the Primary Model: Yi Jing and the Onto-Hermeneutical Tradition," in *Journal of Chinese Philosophy* 30: 3 & 4 (September/December 2003), 289–312.

The Compact Oxford English Dictionary, ed. Murray, Bradley, et al. (New York: Oxford University Press, 1971).

The Cambridge History of Ancient China, ed. Michael Loewe and Edward Shaughnessy (Cambridge: Cambridge University Press, 1998).

Guo Moruo, ed., *Jiaguwen heji* (Beijing: Zhunghua, 1979–1982).

Bernhard Karlgren, *Grammatica Serica Recensa*, reprint from *Museum of Far Eastern Antiquities*, Bulletin No. 29 (Stockholm, 1957).

David Keightley, "The Oracle-Bone Inscriptions of the Late Shang Dynasty," in *Sources of Chinese Tradition (second edition)*, vol. I, compiled by William Theodore deBary and Irene Bloom (New York: Columbia University Press, 1999), 3–20.

Kong Yingda, *Zhouyi zhengyi*, 5: 4a–4b.

Liu Xing-lung, ed., *Xin pien jiagu wen zidian* (Beijing: International Culture Publishing Company, 1993).

Richard John Lynn, *The Classic of Changes: A New Translation of the I Ching as Interpreted by Wang Bi* (New York: Columbia University Press, 1994).

J. P. C. Moffett, *Catalog of Predictions in the Zuozhuan,* supplement to *Prediction in the Zuo-zhuan* (Edinburgh, 1991, unpublished).

Margaret J. Pearson, "Towards a New Reading of Hexagram 44," in *The Oracle: The Journal of Yijing Studies* (London), vol. 2, no. 11 (September 2000), 25–29.

Axel Schuessler, *Minimal Old Chinese and Later Han Chinese, a Companion to Grammata Serica Recensa* (Honolulu: University of Hawai'i Press, 2009).

Edward L. Shaughnessy, "Commentary, Philosophy and Translation: Reading Wang Bi's Commentary to the *Yi Jing* in a New Way," *Early China*: 22, 1997.
_____, *I ching: The Classic of Changes, Translated with an Introduction and Commentary* (New York: Ballantine, 1996).
_____, "Marriage, Divorce, and Revolution: Reading between the Lines of the Book of Changes," in *Before Confucius: Studies in the Creation of the Chinese Classics* (Albany: State University of New York Press, 1997), 13–30.

Shuowen jiezijiju, ed., Jiang Renjie and Liu Rui (Shanghai: Guji, 1996), 79–80, 1907, 2659.

Kidder Smith, "The I Ching Prior to Sung," in *Sung Dynasty Uses of the I Ching*, ed. Kidder Smith, Peter K. Bol, Joseph A. Allen, and Don J. Wyatt (Princeton: Princeton University Press, 1990).

Ssu-ma Ch'ien, *Records of the Grand Historian, vol II, The Age of Emperor Wu,* "Feng and Shan, Biography of the Diviners," tr. Burton Watson (New York: Columbia University Press, 1961), pp 468–475.

Tso chuan: Selections from China's Oldest Narrative History, tr. Burton Watson (New York: Columbia University Press, 1989).

Wang Bi ji jiaoshi (Critical Edition of the works of Wang Bi with explanatory notes), 2 vol. (Beijing: Zhonghua shuji, 1980).

Endymion Wilkinson, "Characters: Evolution and Structure," in *Chinese History: a Manual* (Cambridge: Harvard University Asia Center, 1998), 397–417, esp. 401–414.

Xin pien jiaguwen zidian, ed. Liu Xinglong (Beijing: International Culture Publishing Company, 1993).

Xunzi jianci, ed. Liang Zhexiung (Chungha shuju, Hong Kong, 1974).

Zhang Heng, "A Response to the Earthquakes at the Capital in 133 (*Yangjia ernian jingshi dizhen duici*)," from *HouHanji,* in *Zhang Heng Shiwen jijiaozhu,* Zhang Zhenci, ed. and comm. (Shanghai: Guji chubanci, 1986), 367–368.

Zhang Pingzi [Heng], "Rhapsody on Contemplating the Mystery, Rhapsody on Returning to the Fields" in Xiao Tong, *Wenxuan,* vol. III, tr. David R. Knechtges (Princeton: Princeton University Press, 1996), 104–143.

Zhouyi da cidian, ed. Wu Hua (Canton: Chung-shan [Sun Yat-sen] University Press, 1993).

Appendix

Ox scapulae and turtle and tortoise plastrons were commonly used as oracle bones during the Shang dynasty. Here, an inscribed tortoise plastron dating from the reign of King Wu (late Shang dynasty) shows complementary charges down the outer sides. The cracks formed via the application of heat are numbered 1–6 on the left and 1–7 on the right. The outcome of the interpretation is noted beneath the numbering on the right. (National Museum of China, photograph by BabelStone, printed under the Creative Commons Attribution Share-Alike 3.0 Unported License)

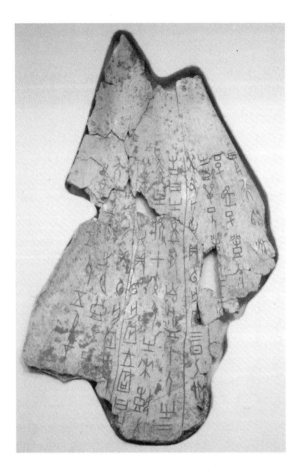

An example of an inscribed ox scapula from the reign of King Wu (late Shang dynasty). Bones and plastrons were the primary material of choice possibly because they offered a large flat area for inscription. (National Museum of China, photograph by Babel-Stone, printed under the Creative Commons Attribution Share-Alike 3.0 Unported License)

Above and on the facing page, bronze oil lamps from the Zhou and Han dynasties. Both figures wear multiple layers of kimonos, tied in place with sashes. Both have long hair, pinned or braided in place. The male figure wears a cap tied under the chin, to hold ends in place and to show his rank, as did some of the terra cotta warriors near the tomb of the First Emperor of Qin. (Cultural Relics Publishing House, Beijing, 1976)

(cont'd) These styles continued for many centuries in China and were adopted, then adapted, by Koreans and Japanese. By the time Europeans arrived in China, successive waves of conquering peoples had changed fashions, though these styles persisted, with some changes, in Japan. (Cultural Relics Publishing House, Beijing, 1976)

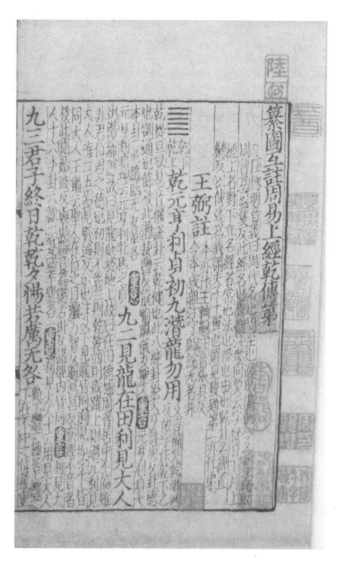

Page of the *I Ching* printed during the Song dynasty (960-1279), using movable type. This is the first page of the text, and shows how the commentary by Wang Bi (d. 249) was often longer than the original text. (See Introduction: "History of the Text" and "Why This Translation? Yin/Yang and Gender")

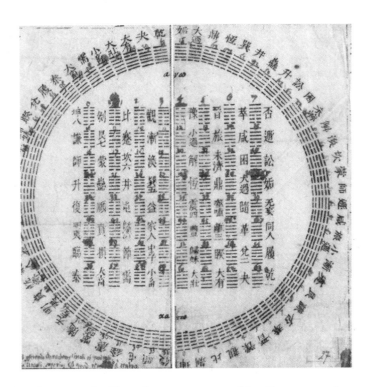

This diagram of I Ching hexagrams owned by German mathematician and philosopher Gottfried Wilhelm Leibniz includes Arabic numerals, faintly visible, added by Leibnitz. The grid in the center shows the hexagrams in the binary (*fuxi*) sequence which fascinated Leibnitz. However, the diagram assumes that the sequence of the received text is the only one, which we now know is not the case. The earlier Mawangdui sequence is quite different, so the deep meanings ascribed to the sequence are suspect. In addition, Leibnitz did not seem to realize that there are not two possibilities for each line, but four. The usual chart showing all hexagrams abbreviates this reality, something not reflected in this diagram or in Leibnitz's belief that this prefigured modern binary analysis. (For more on the six possibilities of each line, see pages 52 to 58)

Depicting a different method of divination, Han dynasty (206 BC – 220 BCE) pottery figures of scholars debating a session of the divination board game *liubo*, whose rules have been lost, but which used a symmetrically patterned board. (Photo by Gary Lee Todd, printed under the Creative Commons Attribution-Share Alike 4.0 International, 3.0 Unported, 2.5 Generic, 2.0 Generic and 1.0 Generic licenses)

The Zhou dynasty gradually replaced Shang usage of ox scapulae and tortoise shells with vegetation: yarrow stalks used for I Ching divination. This was both more humane and less costly. This change spread access to this type of divination from the elite invited to royal banquets to many more, including even peasants who consulted diviners in the marketplaces. When coinage was introduced, the least valuable coins were also used, as most people do today. Both yarrow stalks and low value coins emphasize the words sought rather than the objects used to select them. Some find the longer time needed to use yarrow stalks useful. (Photo by CharlieHuang, printed under the Creative Commons Attribution- Share Alike 4.0 International license.)

From the tomb of Fu Hao (Shang dynasty, c. 1180 BCE). Fu Hao, a wife/consort of King Wu, is known to us through historical records and the artifacts found in her undisturbed tomb when it was first opened in 1976. The weapons and other grave goods found here attest to her roles as a leader of military campaigns and religious rituals in an era when rank and ability apparently outweighed gender. The bird pendant pictured here was old when Fu Hao wore it. Secured by the holes on the. side, it would have swayed when she wore it, though its head would have remained above its body, a fitting symbol for a leader coping with change. This is probably a phoenix, symbol of royal women, as dragons were of royal men. (National Museum of China).

(Most of the hexagrams describe natural phenomena. Only three are about objects made by human beings: the net (30), the well (48) and the ding (20). During the Shange Dynasty, the king gathered his highest-ranking officials for rituals offering feasts to the ancestors and the Lord on High (Shangdi). Bronze vessels were used to hold the meat stews and ales as they were heated over a fire. After the ancestors and deities were served, the king and his guests shared the meal. Note the legs and the "ears" through which a handle could be placed. These are referred to in the hexagram. This ding from the Shanxi Provincial Museum, Taiyuan. (Photo by Gary Todd, printed under the Creative Commons CCO 1.0 Universal Public Domain Dedication).

China's Classical Age: Shang And Zhou Dynasties

SHANG DYNASTY (*c.*1600-1046 BCE)
Bronze age: Ritual vessels and weapons
Writing on oracle bones
Economy: primarily pastoral, then gradual settling
Warfare: walled cities, bronze chariots

ZHOU (Joe) DYNASTY (c. 1046 to 256 BCE)
Government: familial feudalism
Economy: settled agrarian economy, around walled cities

Western Zhou (c.1046 to 771 BCE)
Rulers: "King" Wen (opposed Shang policies)
King Wu (conquered Shang)
King Cheng (infant)
Regent: Duke of Zhou (completed conquest and organized government)
Classics: Book of History, Songs, Changes, Rites, Music

Eastern Zhou (*c.* 770-256 BCE)
Spring and Autumn Period (722-481 BCE) (subject of Confucius's Annals)
Warring States Period (403-221 BCE) ("Hundred Flowers" of differing philosophies)

"Hundred Flowers" of differing philosophies

Confuscians:
Confucius (c. 551-479 BCE)
Mencius (late 4th century BCE)
Xunzi (third century BCE)

Daoists:
Laozi (accounts vary, commonly thought to have lived in the sixth century BCE)
Zhuangzi (late 4th century BCE)

Legalists:
Shang Yang (c. 390-338 BCE)
Han Feizi (c. 280-233 BCE)

QIN DYNASTY (221-207 BCE)
Military/political unification 221 BCE
First Emperor: Qin Shihuangdi (d. 210 BCE)
Prime Minister: Li Si (Legalist) (d. 208 BCE)
Burning of the books (213 BCE)

HAN DYNASTY (206 BCE-220 CE)
Centralized imperial bureaucracy
Imperial University taught Confucian classics

Pronouncing Chinese Names

Vowels:
a = ah as in Shang (Shaang),
Han (Hawn) ei = ay
i = ee
but Shi = sure

Zh = J
Zhou = Joe
Zhuang = Juang

X = Sh
Xin = shin (heart/mind)
Xun = shoon

Zi=dzuh
Kongzi = Confucius or Koong duh
Laozi = Lao-tzu = Lah-ow dzuh (lit.old boy)

The Major Dynasties

Shang (ca. 1600 - 1045? BCE)
Zhou (1045? - 256 BCE)
Qin (221-207 BCE)
Han (206 BCE - 220 CE)
Sui ("sway") (589-617)
Tang (618-906)
Song (960-1279)
Yuan (Mongols)(1279-1367)
Ming (1368-1644)
Qing (Ching) (1644-1911)
Republic (1911-1949 but still continuing on Taiwan)
People's Republic (1949 - present)

About the Poem
on the Facing Page

The greatest political problem facing the creators of the original *Book of Changes* (Zhouyi) was a cruel and unpredictable tyrant. To replace him took many years of preparation, including the marriage of the wise King Wen of the Zhou people to a great and good woman of the Shang lineage. When she came to her future husband's city state, he went beyond protocol to ease her journey, building a bridge for her, and going to meet her. This event is commemorated in this poem, as is the birth and successful life of their son, King Wu, who led the army which finally defeated the tyrant and inaugurated a new dynasty which endured for many centuries.

236. 大明 DA MING

from University of Virginia

The illustration of illustrious [virtue] is required below,
And the dread majesty is on high.
Heaven is not readily to be relied on;
It is not easy to be king.
Yin's rightful heir to the heavenly seat,
Was not permitted to possess the kingdom.

Jin, the second of the princesses of Zhi,
From [the domain of] Yin-shang,
Came to be married to the prince of Zhou,
And because his wife in his capital,
Both she and king Ji,
Were entirely virtuous.
[Then] Da-ren became pregnant,
And gave birth to our king Wen.

This king Wen,
Watchfully and reverently,
With entire intelligence served God,
And so secured the great blessing.

His virtue was without deflection;
And in consequence he received [the allegiance of] the States from
all quarters.

Heaven surveyed this lower world;
And its appointment lighted [on king Wen].
In his early years,
It made for him a mate; –
On the north of the Qia;
On the banks of the Wei.
When king Wen would wive,
There was the lady in a large State.

In a large State was the lady,
Like a fair denizen of Heaven.
The ceremonies determined the auspiciousness [of the union].
And in person he met her on the Wei.
Over it he made a bridge of boats; –
The glory [of the occasion] was illustrious.

The favouring appointment was from Heaven,
Giving the throne to our king Wen,
In the capital of Zhou.
The lady-successor was from Xin,
Its eldest daughter, who came to marry him.
She was blessed to give birth to king Wu,
Who was preserved, and helped, and received also the appointment,
And in accordance with it smote the great Shang.
The troops of Yin-shang,
Were collected like a forest,
And marshalled in the wilderness of Mu.
We rose [to the crisis]; –
'God is with you,' [said Shang-fu to the king],
'Have no doubts in your heart.'

The wilderness of Mu spread out extensive;
Bright shone the chariots of sandal;
The teams of bays, black-maned and white-bellied, galloped along
The grand-master Shang-fu,
Was like an eagle on the wing,
Assisting king Wu,
Who at one onset smote the great Shang.
That morning's encounter was followed by a clear bright [day].

University of Virginia Chinese Text Initiative
https://cti.lib.virginia.edu/shijing/AnoShih.html

*For many centuries, the least valuable Chinese coins were used in
consulting the* Book of Changes. *These coins were round,
to represent the sky surrounding the earth, and had square holes in
the middle, representing the earth. Coins usually carried the reign
name of the ruler. However, these show inscriptions related to this
book. Center coin: the title* Zhouyi *(the* Zhou Dynasty Book of
Changes*). Left coin: an ancient character for yin, as in yin/yang.
Its original meaning is related to birds and topography.
Right coin: an ancient character for woman.*

Consulting the Book of Changes

Two forms

This book helped Carl Jung help his patients, and its rich images have helped rulers and others as they have wrestled with deciding what actions to take. The results of these decisions are documented in the Zuojuan. The great scientist and imperial advisor Zhang Heng described his reactions to his reslts in a long poem.

I have included two blank forms to help readers with two important steps: formulating a good question and recording the results of coin tossing.

Formulating your question

The most effective questions relate to actual actions you are planning to take in the near future. This text can help readers to see situations and relationships which trouble us in fresh ways, and to see more clearly our own preferences. Like any other tool, it works best with some understanding of its likely responses.

We know more about answers to queries than about the queries themselves. But if you look at the lines of the hexagrams, which are intended to be the most direct responses, you will see that the following "answers" are common:

- good fortune
- misfortune
- success
- persistence is effective
- persistence is not effective

These seem to be assessments of planned actions, not responses to vague queries like "What shall I do next?"

So, some preliminary thought will help you form a question that is more useful to you in a number of ways.

First, write down a few words describing the situation or relationship which concerns you.

Recognize that you can only control your own actions and attitudes, not those of others. (Sorry!)

You have probably faced a similar problem in the past. What were some of your strategies then? List a few here:
1.
2.
3.
4.
5.

Pick ONE strategy for one question.

Timing is crucial, as is the sequence of your actions. An action which is appropriate today may not be next week. Select a time dimension: in this calendar year, this month, . . .)

Your question today:

Form 2
(Use with pages 52 to 55.)

Read your question (aloud if possible) and check that it has a defined time.

Now focus on that question alone and pick up three coins of the same kind and shake them in your hands. Let them fall on your table. Write down how many heads and how many tails, below, starting with first toss on the BOTTOM

First hexagram

Second hexagram
(after changes)

heads (x2) tails (x3)

6 ___ equals ___		6)
5 ___ heads (x2) tails (x3) equals___		5)
4 ___ heads (x2) tails (x3) equals___		4)
3 ___ heads (x2) tails (x3) equals___		3)
2 ___ heads (x2) tails (x3) equals___		2)
1 heads (x2) tails (x3) equals		1)

Number of first hexagram
(from chart)

Number of second hexagram after 6 or 9 change and 7 or 8 do not

Use a separate journal or page to copy the texts of your changing lines and the image(s). Write down what you think they mean, including even things that seem contradictory. (Edit later) Read pages 52 to 55 and examples that follow.

Write down your question here:

List some possible actions you could take:

Revise your question to be one of these, preferably either the one you'd prefer or the one you think most likely to be successful.

Be sure that you have specified a time dimension.

On the next page, fill in the question at the top with your edited version.

Now take three coins of the same kind: three pennies or quarters.

Sixth
Fifth
Fourth
Third throw:
Second throw: heads   tails   equals
which looks like
First throw   heads   tails   equals

How to Consult the Changes: Reference Summary

See pages 51-61 for details.

Forming the question
The most effective include a time frame (tomorrow, this month, etc.); are about you, not someone else; are a single question.

Throwing the coins
First throw goes at the bottom, sixth throw at the top.

Determining the hexagrams
- From the numbers thrown, write the first hexagram. Convert it to a second hexagram by copying the stable lines, and changing the changing lines. (If your first hexagram has no changing lines, your result is one hexagram, not two.)
- Use the chart to look up the hexagrams. (Upper trigram appears across top of chart. Lower trigram appears down left side. Where they meet is the hexagram number.)

Considering the hexagrams
- Read the first hexagram: Its name, first statement, any lines for sixes or nines that you have. (Skip the others; they are not yours.) Read the image. Write down the words and your immediate thoughts.
- Read the second hexagram: Its name, first statement, but no lines. Read the image. Write down the words and your thoughts.

Sleep on it. In the morning, reread and write any further insights. Consider. If this is an important decision, consult someone you trust on what this means.

Lower trigram \ Upper trigram	天 Sky	雷 Thunder	水 Water
天 Sky	01	34	05
雷 Thunder	25	51	03
水 Water	06	40	29
山 Mountain	33	62	39
地 Earth	12	16	08
風 Wind	44	32	48
火 Fire	13	55	63
澤 Lake	10	54	60